THE PROSPERITY OF VICE

THE PROSPERITY OF VICE

A Worried View of Economics

DANIEL COHEN
TRANSLATED BY SUSAN EMANUEL

THE MIT PRESS
CAMBRIDGE, MASSACHUSETTS
LONDON, ENGLAND

Originally published as *La prospérité du vice: Une introduction (inquiète) à l'économie* (©
2009 Éditions Albin Michel).

MIT Press books may be purchased at special quantity discounts for business or sales
promotional use. For information, please email special_sales@mitpress.mit.edu or
write to Special Sales Department, The MIT Press, 55 Hayward Street, Cambridge,
MA 02142.

Set in Bembo by Graphic Composition, Inc. Printed and bound in the United States
of America.

Library of Congress Cataloging-in-Publication Data

Cohen, Daniel, 1953–
The prosperity of vice : a worried view of economics / Daniel Cohen ; translated
by Susan Emanuel.
    p. cm.
Includes bibliographical references and index.
ISBN 978-0-262-01730-5 (hardcover : alk. paper)
1. Economics—History. 2. Economics—Sociological aspects. 3. Economic
development. I. Title.
HB75.C64   2012
330—dc23
                                                        2011033365

10   9   8   7   6   5   4   3   2   1

for my gypsy wife

Give me back the Berlin Wall.
Give me Stalin and Saint Paul
I've seen the future, brother:
It is murder.

—*Leonard Cohen*

Contents

INTRODUCTION

What happened yesterday in the West is today being repeated on a world scale. Millions of peasants in China, in India, and elsewhere are leaving the countryside and going to the city. Industrial society is replacing rural society. New powers are emerging. Yesterday it was Germany and Japan; today it is India and China. Rivalries are exacerbated as competition increases for control of raw materials. Financial crises repeat themselves as in the bad old days of capitalism. Contrary to what believers in "the clash of civilizations" maintain, the great risk of the twenty-first century is less a confrontation between cultures and religions than a repetition, at a global level, of the history of the West.

For Europe did not escape the Industrial Revolution unscathed. If today it thinks of itself, despite the current crisis, as the continent of peace and prosperity, it does so at the price of a formidable amnesia about its recent past. With the barbarism of World War II, Europe ended the brief period during which it was the epicenter of human history, a period that had begun in the sixteenth century. Who will bet that Asia will escape such a tragic destiny?

We are sometimes reassured by thinking that prosperity will foster peace, that commercial trade will pacify international relations. Yet it was during a climate of shared prosperity that World War I broke out. It was success that gave Germany self-confidence and worried the other European powers. A retrospective illusion makes us think that peace and prosperity go together. Alas, nothing allows us to be sure of that, and many recent studies point to the opposite.

As Philippe Martin and his co-authors have shown, international trade in no way reduces the risk of wars. According to their study, trade makes it easier for a bellicose nation to attack a rival power. International trade contributes to diversifying the aggressor's sources of supply during the conflict. Neither wealth nor education will make a bad man better. Instead, as the French sociologist Christian Baudelot says, they offer him new ways of staying bad. A well-documented study has analyzed the social origins of perpetrators of terrorist attacks (defined as attacks aimed at civilian populations for political purposes). They are neither poor nor illiterate. Most of them have had higher education. Several (for example, the Italian publisher Giangiacomo Feltrinelli, who died in 1972 while trying to dynamite electricity pylons near Milan) have been millionaires.

These observations run counter to the intuitions underlying the West's view of itself—especially those of Condorcet and Montesquieu, who supposed that education and commerce softened hearts and manners. How could Europe, the seat of a civilization of "well-being," have finished its race in the collective suicide of two world wars? What are the risks that weigh on the non-Western world today, when it is Westernizing?

LAWS HIDDEN SINCE THE ORIGIN OF THE WORLD

Let us begin at the beginning. The law to which societies were long subject before the industrial age was simple and desperate. From the dawn of time until the eighteenth century, the average revenue of the planet's inhabitants remained stagnant. Each time a society began to prosper—because it discovered a new technology, for example—an immutable mechanism went into effect that annulled prosperity's impact. Economic growth entrained demographic growth. Wealth increased the birth rate and reduced the death rate of both infants and adults. But the rise in population gradually lowered per capita revenue. There came the fatal moment when the population ran up against the insufficiency of available land to feed it. Now too numerous, humans died from hunger or sickness. Famines and epidemics invariably broke the rise of growing societies.

Malthus' Law has occasioned the spilling of much ink but ultimately has withstood examination by its critics. Thanks to the work of economic historians, one can estimate in today's currency the average income that prevailed over the centuries. The living standard of a Roman slave was not significantly different from that of a peasant in the Languedoc in the seventeenth century or that of a worker in major industry at the start of the nineteenth century. It was close to that of a poor person in the modern world: around a dollar a day. The economic historian Gregory Clark presents fascinating evidence of this long stagnation. Life expectancy remained close to 35 years throughout human history, both for hunter-gatherers (who can be observed today in aboriginal societies) and for the earliest workers in modern industry at the dawn of the nineteenth century. Examination of skeletons also shows that material conditions (as measured by body size) weren't greatly different in the era of hunter-gatherers than at the dawn of the nineteenth century.

Malthus' Law invalidates the usual categories of good and evil. For example, life in Tahiti was heavenly, but thanks to a high incidence of infanticide. More than two-thirds of newborns were instantly killed by smothering them, strangling them, or breaking their necks. Everything that contributes to increasing mortality proves to be a good thing because it reduces competition for available land. Public hygiene, inversely, works against societies that respect it. The European person was on average richer than the Chinese person at the start of the eighteenth century, because he was dirty. To his great benefit, the European did not bathe, whereas the Chinaman or the Japanese washed as often as possible. Europeans, whatever their social class, did not see anything wrong with toilets adjacent to their habitations, despite the odors. The Japanese were, in comparison, absolute models of cleanliness. Their streets were regularly washed, and they removed their shoes before entering a home. This explains why they were more numerous—and poorer. This was the reign of the prosperity of vice.

At the Origins of European Supremacy

Humanity owes to Europe the discovery of the Philosopher's Stone: the possibility of perpetual growth, not only of the population but also of the average income. That discovery did not happen all at once. It was the fruit of a slow evolution that stretched from the twelfth century to the eighteenth, a period the medievalist Jacques Le Goff characterized as the "long Middle Ages." Economic growth came to rely on a permanent technological revolution, and it would overwhelm demographic growth. From the nineteenth century on, in industrialized countries, it was growth in per capita income that became the mark of a prosperous society. Growth (ultimately) improved living conditions, and lengthened life spans instead of reducing them. The postponement of death is the great novelty of the modern era.

Thousands of pages have been written on what happened, and it remains the subject of furious controversies. Why was it in Europe that the possibility of perpetual growth was discovered? China seemed a better prospect. Francis Bacon considered the three fundamental inventions of the modern world to be the compass, the printing press, and gunpowder. But all three were invented in China. A century before Columbus equipped his three ships, a much more impressive fleet, commanded by Admiral Zhang He, was skirting the African coasts and bringing zebras and giraffes to the emperor's court.

Why did Chinese dynamism stall? There were several factors, but one of them would be decisive. Abruptly, the emperor decided that overseas voyages were costly and useless. The search for domestic stability became a priority for him, and exploration of the world was demoted. The emperor had the fleet's ships burned. China lost its maritime ascendancy and its taste for long-distance commerce, and sank into immobility.

While China sacrificed growth for the sake of domestic stability, Europe took the opposite path, less by choice than as a result of competition among nations. Gunpowder remained a plaything in China, but in Europe it became an effective weapon of war. To get powder into a cannon required a series of delicate inventions, stimulated in each country by the advances of its competitors. In the realm of ideas, political fragmentation also played a decisive role. Galileo's curiosity was condemned by the Church, but science rebounded in the anti-papist England of Newton. Columbus had to make several tours of European capitals before finding a sponsor for his exploration.

But at the heart of European dynamism was a poison that would cause its demise. An immutable cycle was in place. Each time one power tried to dominate the others, it unleashed a coalition of all the others to defeat it. Thus Europe was successively dominated by Spain in the sixteenth century, Holland in the seventeenth, France in the eighteenth, and England in the nineteenth. The twentieth was supposed to have been the German century, which in a sense it was. World War I wasn't an "accident" along Europe's journey; it was its logical outcome.

Someone who wants to understand the multi-polar world that is burgeoning in the twenty-first century need only look at the European history of which he or she is now an heir. All countries are now nation-states, on the model invented in Europe. Each people is "emperor" inside its own borders, furiously jealous of those borders. The first fragility of the world to come is played out there. The emerging powers, now armed with unprecedented wealth and military power procured by industrialization, are trying to settle their ancient quarrels over borders and precedence.

ADDICTION TO GROWTH

Not only does industrialization overthrow the equilibrium of power among countries; it also radically transforms the internal functioning of societies. In the famous words of the Austrian-American economist Joseph Schumpeter, capitalism is a process of *"creative destruction* that is constantly revolutionizing the economic structure from inside, by continually destroying its outmoded elements and by continually creating new elements." This is why industrial societies are fragile entities that require constant care. They mingle creation and destruction, they alternate prosperity and depression, and they nearly collapsed from battering of the crisis of 1929 (of which the subprime crisis of the late 2000s was a brutal reminder).

If prosperity was at the origin of World War I, the dislocation of German society as an effect of the great crisis of the 1930s explains World War II. And it is difficult to plead that the 1929 crisis was an accident. The subprime crisis recapitulated the same mechanisms, the same sequence of events, even though the lessons of the 1930s had strongly influenced the postwar years and a world more inclined to cooperation had appeared since then. Western nations, devastated after 1945 and united by the Cold War, had defused their own conflicts. The welfare state had softened the struggle between classes, and in Europe the "social market economy" prospered. But the energy crisis of the 1970s, the fall of the Berlin Wall, and the financial revolution of the 1980s marked the end of this postwar sequence. The consensus manufactured in the 1950s and the 1960s dwindled and then died. And in less than three decades, the crisis came back.

The question posed by the subprime crisis goes beyond the regulation of markets. It also raises questions about the so-called moral regulation of capitalism. Crazy money, coming back in the windfalls of the 1980s, gave credence to Marx's accusation that the bourgeoisie drowned society in "the icy water of egotistical calculation." American households' greed to consume, a cause of their impressive indebtedness and the principal factor in the subprime crisis, raises the issue of the values and frustrations underlying capitalism.

The Malthusian man was constantly hungry, in the literal sense. Wars and epidemics were good in that they reduced the number of mouths to be fed. Is the modern world's victory over hunger and abject poverty a sign of the revenge of virtue over vice? Unfortunately, nothing is less certain. Competition for available land gave way to a social rivalry that has been democratized by modern economic growth. Modern humans remain greedy, but they are greedy for goods of whose existence they were ignorant a few years ago. As the French demographer Alfred Sauvy said, the modern person is a walker who never reaches the horizon. Whatever the pleasures already satisfied, the page always remains blank for those who want to be satisfied. Consumption has become a drug, an addiction. The pleasure is ephemeral.

As the economist Richard Easterlin has shown (relying on a number of studies), rich societies are not happier than poor ones. What matters is to do better than others. As a nineteenth-century humorist cited by *The Economist* put it, "to be happy is to earn ten dollars more than your brother-in-law." Rapid growth does ease social tensions, since everyone can believe that he is catching up. But this ideal is vulnerable to any slowing of growth, whatever the level of wealth already achieved. France was thus incomparably happier during the Thirty Glorious Years—the decades of crazy growth after World War II—than it is today. The disillusionment felt by rich countries when growth slows will necessarily hit the newly emergent countries when they discover its meaning for themselves.

THE HOUR OF GLOBALIZATION

Some argue that the unhealthy addiction of *homo consumerus* to growth also explains why growth remains strong, which would ultimately be a good thing. Perhaps. But the consequences of this insatiable appetite are posed in unprecedented terms in the era of globalization. That a billion Chinese consume a billion bicycles carries no ecological consequences. As Adam Smith might say, everybody wins—those who sell them and those who buy them. But if the Chinese consume a billion *cars*, everything changes; the future of the planet is threatened, and the worst is to be feared. As early as 2050, the concentration of CO_2 in the atmosphere may be twice what it was in the pre-industrial age. Modern economic growth runs up against a formidable obstacle: not the rarity of arable land (as in Malthus' time), but the fragility of the whole ecosystem.

At a time when a devouring material civilization is being propagated all over the planet, another rupture with the past is also at work. The West is engaged (and entrains the rest of the world) in a transition toward what has been called the "cyber-world." This new virtual space is the theater of the new and immaterial globalization borne by information and communication technologies. No planetary congestion is to be feared in this domain—exactly the opposite. The larger the human population, the more the cyber-world prospers. The production of new ideas or works of the mind flourishes all the more thanks to the number of researchers and artists who participate. The nationality of the person who finds a vaccine against AIDS will not matter; he or she will have produced a planetary good. China has 60 million pianists; its chances of producing a new Mozart are commensurate with that figure. When that day comes, everyone will gain. In the political domain, the idea of democracy crosses all borders, thanks much more to the circulation of ideas than to the circulation of merchandise.

Immaterial globalization has only just begun. Far from being a pacified space, the new space of world communication is as full of love *and* hatred as the old one. Flourishing on the Internet are as many links among music lovers as among pedophiles and terrorists. Everyone's "fifteen minutes of fame" (as promised by Andy Warhol) becomes a new horizon of expectation, a horizon just as remote for the young who frequent Facebook-type social networks as for those who are attracted to al-Qaeda.

Still, the grand hope of the twenty-first century is the creation within this cyber-world of a new awareness of the solidarity that now links us all together. At the moment of ecological risk, humanity can no longer labor under the laws of Malthus or Easterlin, which it does not understand or which it understands too late. To grasp how the laws of economics fashion history, and to understand how, in turn, history transforms the supposedly inflexible laws of economics— this is the goal of the journey through the past and the future that I propose to undertake in this book, standing on the shoulders of the giants of economic thought: Adam Smith, Karl Marx, John Maynard Keynes, Joseph Schumpeter, and Albert Hirschman.

I

WHY THE WEST?

Genesis

The Birth of the Economy

For a long time, humankind's sole problem was feeding itself. From the dawn of time until the invention of agriculture (only 10,000 years ago), men and women fed themselves by taking freely what nature offered. Hunting and gathering, two activities that are not socially exacting, sufficed. Then, almost all at once, humankind learned to cultivate the earth and to make its flocks increase. This is the moment when—to parody Jean-Jacques Rousseau—people realized you could enclose a field and say "This is mine."

How did this Neolithic revolution take place? The customary thesis comes from the Australian anthropologist Gordon Childe and attributes the discovery of agriculture to a "natural" cause. Climatic warming abruptly destroyed fauna and game, creating a shortage that pushed man to search for other ways of feeding himself. Agriculture would have been the daughter of necessity. Man then went on to transform his way of living. He became sedentary and invented gods of the seasons and rainfall to accompany his new existence as a farmer.

But recent work relying on precise carbon-14 dating has overturned this interpretation. For Jacques Cauvin, in a striking book titled *The Birth of the Gods and the Origins of Agriculture*,[1] it seems that sedentariness *preceded* the invention of agriculture. The first town in human history, Jericho, predates the first cultivation of wheat. This discovery alone would suffice to show that animals and game were abundant enough to allow humans to become sedentary. Therefore, at the end of the tenth millennium before our era, the assembling of humans stemmed from a social factor, not from economic and demographic ones.

If sedentariness preceded the Neolithic period, it would seem the same is true for belief in divinities. This thesis is more difficult to prove. How can we show the precedence of a belief? Prehistorians establish it by noting, first, that the practice of burying the dead precedes the Neolithic by several thousand years. Then they point out that on the eve of the Neolithic humans gradually abandoned representing animals alone and depicted figures (most often female) that resemble images of gods. The only animal figure was now that of the bull. But the wild bullock was not yet a game animal, as the gazelle was. Therefore it probably had a new symbolic value. Later, the figures of the woman and the bull became associated. The woman would be represented giving birth to the bull. This image accompanied the dissemination of the Neolithic from the Middle East to other societies.

No longer mere victims of nature, humans established a new role for themselves. Their having been created by the gods authorized them to be creators in turn. Cauvin summarizes the transformation as follows: "This new chasm which was formed between god and man is dynamic in effect. . . . It must have completely modified the portrayal that the human spirit makes of itself, and, through some kind of release of the necessary energy to see them through, it must also have stimulated new initiatives, like the countervailing effect of an existential malaise never previously experienced."[2] Until then spectators of nature, Neolithic societies were now able to intervene as active producers. Religion gave access to a sort of "transcendental logic" that humankind then applied to the real world.

These dazzling achievements shed new light on things that had been thought unknowable. Did man think in advance of the world in which he was later going to evolve, or should we accept that agriculture, without preliminaries and by chance, overturned human existence? Cauvin's argument is that man first had to modify his frameworks of thought. Obviously this doesn't mean that the consequences of the agricultural revolution (including the birth of empires) were understood beforehand. A gap (which would become considerable) yawned between the intuition of a world to come and the reality that would arise—a reality that humans would find hard to grasp for this very reason. This gap illuminates the difficulty we will encounter when we come to apprehend another great rupture in human history: the Industrial Revolution. Far from appearing as an abrupt break, springing forth fully formed in the middle of the eighteenth century, it too should be understood as an effect of a slow mutation, which had to be thought of before coming into existence, before getting away from the idea of it held by those who had first imagined it.

The first globalization

Agriculture wasn't invented only in the Middle East. It also was invented in China (around 7500 BCE), in Meso-America and in the Andes (around 3500 BCE), and in the east of North America (around 2500 BCE). It is difficult to know if all these discoveries were made autonomously or if they were imported from one region to another. In any case, agriculture took hold almost everywhere from the moment its existence was uncovered.

According to prehistorians, the Neolithic revolution progressed across the Middle East at the average rate of three miles per year, carrying with it the gods who came from the banks of the Jordan. The goddess-and-bull duo touched regions where nothing previously indicated that people had adopted the Neolithic revolution.

A form of social Darwinism is at work here. One technology that is more productive than another almost always tends to take hold, either through persuasion or by force—through persuasion when those who had been deprived of it discovered its potential rather early, and by force because societies of farmers, better nourished and more numerous, rarely missed an opportunity to exterminate societies of hunter-gatherers that they encountered.

There are some counter-examples of societies that resisted. Australian aborigines, while trading with neighboring farmers, have managed for a long time to preserve their societies of hunting and gathering. But they are the exceptions to a rule that, for want of anything better, we might call "the tyranny of productivity."

The first technological explosion

The propagation of agriculture overthrew the framework of human life. The population grew considerably. A nomadic society is curtailed demographically, one simple reason being that a mother must wait until her infant can walk before having another. A sedentary society can have as many children as the land can feed. Agricultural productivity was suddenly augmented, and sedentary living accelerated the population increase. There were about 10 million humans when agriculture came along, about 200 million when Christ was born.

Abundance and staying put also allowed the stockpiling of food. Surplus enabled the feeding of a "sterile class" (as it was called much later by the first modern economists, the Physiocrats, under the reign of Louis XV of France). Kings, their bureaucracies, priests, and warriors gradually became detached from the peasants. Between the Neolithic and the Iron Age, this separation made possible a real leap forward in technology. Blacksmiths in Asia Minor invented bronze around 3500 BCE and iron around 1000 BCE. Bureaucrats invented writing around 3000 BCE in Sumer and around 1300 BCE in China. Greek poets invented vowels around 800 BCE. Between 1300 and 1100 BCE, the hammering of bronze to make vases, helmets, breastplates, and shields became a widely practiced technique. We are now on the threshold of the world that we know through Homer's *Iliad*.

Often a discovery was made several times over, as with writing or bronze. Sometimes one example was copied by societies that were in contact with the inventor, as with the alphabet. The horse, originally found in only one place (the Ukraine), ran across the world, bearing on its back warriors to whom it gave a decisive advantage.

These discoveries would bring increasing social complexity to human societies. Fiefdoms became kingdoms and then empires. The great civilizations of Sumeria, Egypt, Minoa, India, and China were born in the wake of these inventions. One among them, Western civilization, assumed ascendancy over the others starting in the sixteenth century. Why?

———

7

The Broken Destiny of the West

Why, of all the civilizations on earth, was it ultimately the West that outdistanced the others and imposed its model on the rest? In a comparison between Europe just after the year 1000 and the Arab world or China, any technological advantage certainly would not go to the West. What happened?

The Greco-Roman civilization from which the Christian West was born was brilliant. Rome in 100 BCE was better equipped with paved roads, sewers, foodstuffs, and water than most European capitals in 1800. The Romans deployed exceptional ingenuity in architecture (they discovered cement) and in road building. They inherited tools the Greeks had refined, including levers, screws, pulleys, and gears—innovations that would enable them to fabricate effective weapons.

But civilian use of these technologies remained dormant for millennia. In everything that directly touched economic life, the period from 500 BCE to 500 CE was impoverished in the West. From a strictly technological viewpoint, according to the historian Joel Mokyr, ancient Greco-Roman society did nothing very inventive with tools.[3] It constructed water wheels but did not really use hydraulic energy. It mastered the manufacture of glass and understood how to use the sun's rays, but did not invent eyeglasses. In comparison with the great leap that occurred between the Neolithic and the Iron Age with the development of fundamental procedures of agriculture, metallurgy, ceramics, and weaving, there was a slowdown under the Greco-Roman Empire. In the agricultural realm, it lagged behind the great irrigation projects of Egypt and Mesopotamia. Industrial progress in the West during

Antiquity and the Middle Ages lagged far behind the progress achieved in China.

As the historian of antiquity Aldo Schiavone puts it, "the famed Roman 'pragmatism' was social, not technological. It affected matters of government, politics, law, and military organization. . . . None of the great engineers and architects, none of the incomparable builders of bridges, roads, and aqueducts, none of the experts in the employment of the apparatus of war, and none of their customers, either in the public administration or in the large landowning families, understood that the most advantageous arena for the use and improvement of machines . . . would have been farms and workshops."[4]

Here Rome inherited the Greek tradition. For the Greeks, what constituted freedom was mastery of the techniques of social life: writing and its rules, music and poetry, knowledge of oneself, and so on. Greek society invented the city as the site of politics, and did not transform the astronomical techniques of Egypt and Chaldea into an experimental science but into metaphysics. "The technological advances that allowed the creation of that civilization," Schiavone writes, "were now disregarded, becoming the shadowy side of this world. To ignore them was the revenge of thought that was finally liberated from past constraints."[5]

Slavery

Aristotle said that one was a master or a slave "by nature." Behind the figure of the slave lay the whole idea of work, which gradually became incomprehensible to the Romans. For a cultivated Roman, it was quite normal that a slave should work the whole day under tight surveillance, that he should possess not the slightest privacy, and that his food should be limited to the amount necessary to sustain his strength. This hardship wasn't specific to Roman civilization or even to societies that kept slaves; it was found in many pre-industrial societies. Generations of peasants in medieval Europe and British workers at the start of the Industrial Revolution paid a human price just as heavy.

But one factor played a decisive role in the transformation of Rome into the capital of servitude. With the first wars against Carthage, the Punic Wars, a mass of slaves such as had never been seen in the ancient West began to be used in a regular way. There were about 600,000 of them in Italy around 225 BCE, in a population that could not have been larger than 4 million. Schiavone quotes Quintus to the effect that the Romans first became aware of the benefits of their wealth when they made themselves masters of this population.

This dynamic was strengthened with the conquests of Pompey and then Caesar. Thanks to the dominance Rome regained on the seas, there was a new influx of slaves. Under Augustus, at the end of the first century before Christ, slaves made up at least 35 percent of the population of Italy. Buying a slave in Imperial Rome didn't cost much: from 1,000 to 2,000 sesterces, at a time when a patrimonial estate easily reached tens of millions of sesterces. Between the second and the first century BCE, thousands and thousands of prisoners were given to merchants who followed the troops and fed the slave market.

Bur revolts were frequent, not only on the great agricultural estates (latifundia) but also, and especially, in the mines. Each generation had its insurrection. The most significant and most famous was that of Spartacus, which also entrained some free men belonging to the lowest social strata. When it was crushed, 6,000 slaves were tortured and crucified on the route from Capua to Rome. After that definitive lesson, there were no more major revolts.

The constantly more intense and regular use of great numbers of men reduced to servitude undermined the situation of small rural property owners. The great estates of the Roman aristocracy swelled. For the small farmer, the only open avenue was to become a professional soldier. A self-sustaining mechanism was set up. Slavery broke small farm holdings, which pushed small landowners to enlist as soldiers and to maintain the mechanism of war spoils, which increased the number of slaves and reduced the number of smallholders. But this evolution also resulted in extensive unemployment in the major cities, where the disinherited from the countryside took refuge.

This dynamic was finally interrupted in the second century, when war stopped being an investment and assumed a purely defensive character. The dynamic of expansion was broken. Between the start and the middle of the second century, the imbalance between resources and needs took the form (including in the awareness of contemporaries) of a veritable "historic collapse." The decline of the Roman Empire had begun.

The West would have to march backward to get out of the impasse into which the Roman system had led it. Schiavone concludes that, as a result of persisting in depending on slavery and refusing the social and intellectual development of labor, hence continuing to confine the space of production to irremediable marginality, "all that was left was a blind alley leading toward a society without growth, structurally incapable of producing innovation and development. It was like a dead letter in history."[6]

———

The Birth of the Modern World

The European Miracle

In the tenth century, Europe seemed to have lost everything that had constituted the glory of Rome and Athens. It had lost the essential part of its scientific knowledge, and had regressed to an almost autarkic situation. When it wanted to buy foreign goods, slaves were often all it could export. Five hundred years later, everything had changed. The Asiatic explorations of Vasco da Gama and the "discovery" of America opened the way to domination of the planet by the West, which would last five centuries. What happened? Let us take up the thread of these unexpected transformations.

In the tenth century, the countryside was still inward-looking, haunted by threats from the Vikings in the north, from the Muslim and Hungarian pillagers to the south and east, and from rural brigands in the center. The circulation of merchandise and persons was reduced to almost nothing. An isolated castle stronghold constituted a whole rural society. As the sociologist Henri Mendras writes in *The End of the Peasantry*, "Carolingian Europe was entirely rural. There were no cities, only farm regions populated by peasants grouped in villages around the manors of the *seigneurs*."[7] This gave the *seigneurs* a monopoly over violence, which enabled them to appropriate the agricultural surplus. Deductions were made in kind. The richest had to travel from one castle to another to consume *in situ* the wine and hunting game that were due them.

At the end of the tenth century, and through a first Renaissance (the eleventh, twelfth, and thirteenth centuries), the almost autarkic unity of the Middle Ages gradually subsided. The Viking threat dissipated, and roads became usable once more.[8] Trade in merchandise and movement of people were again possible.

Rising agricultural productivity was one of the major aspects of the medieval revival. The area of cultivated land increased; so did the population. Tools multiplied and became more effective. Shovels, spades, and plows were now made of iron; harrows appeared; horse harnesses and water mills spread. The improvement in agricultural productivity made it possible to store surpluses that would literally feed the expansion.

The urban and commercial revolution that took place between the eleventh century and the thirteenth put towns back at the center of European history. Some of these town were new, among them Venice, Ferrara, and Amalfi. The old towns that managed to revive rested on entirely new bases. The great ancient cities had been places of consumption more than places of production. None could be defined as an "industrial city." The towns of the Middle Ages, in contrast, were full of artisans. Bells chiming the hours set the rhythm of their lives.

———

Work gradually moved away from the framework in which the ancient world had confined it. Work ceased being the penitential work of the Bible and the High Middle Ages and gradually became a "means of salvation." As the medievalist Jacques Le Goff put it, from the first half of the fourteenth century on, "to waste one's time became a grave sin, a spiritual scandal."[9] This mutation in work was certainly not general. Simple work wasn't appreciated. As Le Goff notes, "a split occurred in the thirteenth century between manual work, more despised than ever, and 'intellectual' work, that of the merchant and the scholar." Around 1400, the new man was a humanist, and foremost an Italian humanist—a merchant who transposed the organization of his business into daily life, regulating his use of time. This break upset the rhythm of the agrarian economy, a rhythm "exempt from haste, without concern for exactitude, without worry over productivity—and of a society in its image, sober and modest, without great appetites, demanding little, scarcely capable of quantitative effort."

The rise of the modern world

The number of inventions produced or imported between the twelfth century and the eighteenth is stupefying: Gothic architecture, pendulum clocks, paper, printing presses, eyeglasses, musical instruments, quality textiles, and so on. If such inventions had little impact on economic growth as a whole, it was because they long remained luxury goods reserved for a small number of users. At first the printing press affected only the few people who knew how to read—largely, of course, because before Gutenberg it was difficult to obtain a book.

To measure the general import of these innovations, Gregory Clark reconstituted notional growth using schemas of "modern" consumption, weighting sectors according to their shares in nineteenth-century spending instead of using thirteenth-century weightings, and concluded that growth was much stronger than had been thought. According to this method, per capita income would have increased 300 percent between the medieval period and 1880. Production of books alone increased by 1 percent a year between the sixteenth century and the eighteenth, so that the old offering of 120 manuscripts a year shot up to 20 million printed books in 1790.[10] The gap between the growth of modern sectors serving an elite and overall growth shows in passing that the great innovations of this period were principally guided not by the search for profit but rather by the curiosity of the inventors, by their appetite for knowledge.

The history of European philosophic and scientific thought from the fifteenth century to the seventeenth is punctuated by stunning advances. In 1543, Copernicus published *De revolutionibus orbium*. In 1644 Descartes' *Principia philosophiae* appeared, and in 1687 Newton's *Principia Mathematica*. Science instituted a new unity between basic research and technology. The Greeks had mastered Ptolemy's astronomy but had never imagined putting it to useful purposes—navigation, for example. They thought it was possible to understand the movement of the stars, but not the trajectory of a stone.[11] The Greeks and the Romans had ignored both the possibility of recognizing the perceived world as a territory of reason and the possibility of dominating and controlling it by means of experimental verification. The new spirit of Bacon and Descartes goes back to the end of the Middle Ages, to the start of the Renaissance, but scarcely beyond that.[12]

As Alexander Koyré puts it in his book *From the Closed World to the Infinite Universe*, the new science was characterized by "study of the phenomena of Nature by means of experiments and rational mechanics."[13] The astonishing conjunction of pure reasoning and experimentation was, as Einstein said, the improbable miracle of the science of Newton and Galileo.

From a latter-day viewpoint the scientific revolution was an incomparable blessing, but those who witnessed it experienced it as a break with the past that was both marvelous and painful. As Koyré also says, the toppling of the conception of the universe as a mathematical space, both infinite and void, meant that "human (or at least the European) minds underwent a deep revolution which changed the very framework and patterns of our thinking and of which modern science and modern philosophy are, at the same time, the root and the fruit. . . . This 'crisis of European consciousness' has been explained in many different ways . . . by some historians as . . . the alleged conversion of the human mind from *theoria* to *praxis*, which transformed man from a spectator into an owner and master of nature . . . ; still others have simply described the despair and confusion brought by the 'new philosophy' into a world from which all coherence was gone and in which the skies no longer announced the glory of God."[14] Whatever the pain of this birthing, modern man and woman, with their doubts and their expectations, had come into the world.

THE BALANCE OF POWER

No theory will ever set straight, on its own, the causes that figured in the origin of the path that Europe took between the twelfth century

---

and the eighteenth. It seems indisputable that the void caused by the disappearance of the Roman Empire, followed by the rivalry between the new European powers to occupy the vacant space, would play an essential role in the evolution of Europe's political, economic, and moral personality.

The notion of a balance of power is generally associated with the Treaty of Utrecht, signed in 1713, which sealed a compromise among France, Britain, and Spain. However, it was at the heart of the political dynamic from the beginning, from the division of the Holy Roman Empire among Charlemagne's heirs in 843. With each king wanting to be "emperor in his own kingdom," this permanent competition among states explains the immutable cycle of war and peace to which Europe was constantly subject.

The economic historian Eric Jones notes in his book *The European Miracle* that geography offers a possible explanation for Europe's political trajectory.[15] Its natural borders—the Alps, the Pyrenees, the Channel—explain the difficulty of constituting a new empire after the fall of the Roman Empire. The defenses these borders offered to England, Spain, and to a lesser extent France explain why those three nations managed to attain greater political stability than Germany, Austria, or Poland. Europe's position at the periphery of Eurasia also protected it from the Mongols. While Baghdad, Damascus, and other Muslim cities were annihilated by the successors of Genghis Kahn, and this threat would remain constantly at the heart of Chinese preoccupations, fear of the Mongols would disappear, slowly but surely, from the European imagination.

The history of wars on the continent provides a guide to the transformations that would occur. In the Middle Ages, any vassal

―――――

owed a payment in kind to his sovereign lord. For a period of 40 days, he put at the lord's disposal a certain number of knights, who were freed from any obligation each 41st day. The development of the monetary economy that accelerated in the eleventh, twelfth, and thirteenth centuries allowed a vassal to substitute a payment in currency for this payment in kind. This monetary financing absolved monarchs of the vicissitudes to which the 40-day system led, and allowed them to mount regular armies. A lord could thus recruit mercenaries. Specialists of all kinds—English archers, Swiss pikemen, Genevan harquebusiers, and so on—would gradually cause the feudal army to disappear.

The new military technology gave the advantage to better-equipped and more innovative armies. In the Battle of Crecy (1346), the English already had bombards that threw projectiles against the enemy but whose main effect was to frighten the horses. A century later, after many improvements, cannons threatened fortified castles. The security that lords could offer their people disappeared under the threat of their shots. Between 1450 and 1550, local lords had to face the fact that fortifications, even improved ones, no longer could protect them. Only royal power could provide security.

In the economic domain, feudalism recoiled before the great bubonic plague of the fourteenth century, a plague that reduced Europe's population by about one-third. The sudden scarceness of people in relation to land gave peasants a new freedom. It allowed them to leave overly exigent lords and to seek refuge elsewhere, assured of being welcomed by other lords who lacked manpower. In "Europe of the West" (meaning west of the Elbe River), most peasants became free after 1500. They could legally marry, migrate, and become owners of land. The feudal system was undermined, and kings would now extend their protection to peasants, undermining the authority of seigniorial justice even more.[16]

The great schism between Eastern and Western Europe dates from this rupture. In the east, peasants lost the battle for their emancipation. The ruling class forced them back in line, exploiting them brazenly, without every trying to make innovations. Thus it was not until the end of the nineteenth century that slavery was abolished in Russia.

The civilizing of manners

Between the middle of the sixteenth century and the middle of the seventeenth there was a strange period of violence, surgically studied by the French historian Robert Muchembled.[17] Blood flowed. Henry III and Henry IV of France and other kings were assassinated. There were countless religious wars. The extreme disorganization of the continent led to incessant rivalry between competing churches and between ambitious princes. Many armies plowing through European lands inflicted horrors on the vanquished, including the civilian population. But the silent consequence of this general movement was to push all states, more or less quickly, to try to disarm and to pacify those of their citizens who were neither soldiers nor guardians of the order.

Commanded to stop bearing arms, people sought the protection that would be guaranteed by royal justice. Marshals, bailiffs, and a career army lodged in barracks took over from mercenaries. A philosophical effort was undertaken to distinguish common violence from "legitimate" violence, which implied strictly limiting the right to kill to what was motivated by sacred duty to the country, to loved ones, and to legitimate self-defense. In the middle of the seventeenth century, the murder statistics began a long decline. What the German sociologist Norbert Elias called "the civilizing of manners" began.[18]

Resisters were eliminated pitilessly. From 1768 to 1772, according to Muchembled, the French constabulary—reputedly the best in Europe—arrested 71,760 beggars, many of them rootless and hopeless young men from the countryside. Thanks to that roundup, homicide ceased being the authorities' main worry. Now law enforcement's target was theft. "Simple theft, or, for servants the act of stealing the least thing from their master, even just a handkerchief, could lead to the gallows." Starting in the middle of the eighteenth century, secure ownership of goods became essential. Bourgeois civilization was preparing to dominate the world.

The birth of representative democracy

In nations in turmoil over these changes, a new regulatory principle was arising, though it was fragile at the start. In most European countries, in the fourteenth century, assemblies began to appear under various names: Estates General, Cortes, Parliament. They had common characteristics and answered the same need: to face directly the budgetary needs of states.[19]

No place demonstrates the originality of the process better than England. Barons who marched on London in May 1214 obtained from "Landless" King John a reversal of his decision to levy an exceptional tax that exempted only the barons who had accompanied him to France. John had to back down and grant the Magna Carta, a document that anticipated the French Declaration of the Rights of Man by several centuries. The barons obtained a promise from the king to ensure impartial justice and to guarantee individual liberties. But the fiscal question was at the heart of the text. The king had to submit any increase in taxes to the consent of the parliament. Representative democracy was born.

Always consulted thereafter, the English Parliament maintained and strengthened its legitimacy.[20] When the Stuarts had to find solutions to their financial difficulties in the middle of the seventeenth century, they had to face an assembly whose help was all the more necessary because the kingdom did not possess effective fiscal administration. Two revolutions (one in 1648, one in 1688) would be necessary to fix the balance between this new power and that of the king. In 1689, the thirteen articles of the Declaration of Rights consecrated the fiscal power adumbrated in the Magna Carta. The king could raise neither taxes nor an army without the help of Parliament.[21]

This oversight of the kingdom's finances proved very good news for fiscal administration. It reassured bankers and allowed state borrowing to benefit from a significant lowering in interest rates, which would tumble from 9 percent on average before 1688 to 3 percent in 1750. According to the economist Douglas North, this turn of events was decisive. Britain owed its economic success to the "best of institutions": better respect for private property and better protection against the risk of expropriation—both guarantees of which Parliament was a vigilant guardian.[22]

The idea that democracy lowered interest rates has been criticized by many historians. One can show that the rate of interest paid by the private sector increased rather than decreased after the English Revolution, long remaining at the level of homologous European nations. But it was the rates on commercial transactions that would

---

matter in the financing of investment and the accumulation of capital.[23] The idea that the Glorious Revolution of 1688 launched the development of capitalism doesn't stand up to examination.

In fact, it was with respect to the military rivalry with France that the low interest rates paid on public debt would give England a decisive advantage. After the costly war England and France waged during the American War of Independence, England could comfortably finance its military expenses through borrowing, while France wallowed in financial difficulty and had to refinance a heavier and heavier debt. Like emergent countries that today must appeal to the International Monetary Fund to solve their problems, Louis XVI had to hand over the management of French public finances to the Swiss banker Necker. Having to convene the Estates General to resolve the state's budgetary problems was how Louis XVI lost his head. The same had happened to King Charles of the House of Stuart.

Conclusion

Europe invented a new political model, that of the nation-state. It was midway between the two great previous models: the city (with Athens as the perfect example and Venice, Florence, and the Hanseatic lands as successors) and the empire (with Rome as the model). The empire had long remained in the European consciousness as a powerful fiction; for example, the Germanic Roman Empire wasn't formally abolished until 1806. But no European power would ever manage to restore imperial order. Each would learn to live within its own borders, in competition with neighbors situated on the other side of a sea or a mountain. This permanent tension would be one of the foundations of European dynamism. Europe had to learn to conjugate the idea of a universal empire, present through the Christian faith especially, with the singular genius of each nation.

It was at the intersection of these military and moral tensions that humanist and scientific thought managed to prosper. The trial of Galileo (1633) stifled Italian science for a while, but the flame passed without difficulty to the England of Newton. No idea, no matter how revolutionary, could be stifled for long. An idea would always find favor with a king or a prince who was tempted to checkmate his neighbor. The commercial culture spread from Genoa to Antwerp and Amsterdam to London. Before obtaining funding for his voyage to the Indies, Christopher Columbus (himself from Genoa) toured Europe's capitals several times. All refused to finance him. At last he obtained his funding from Spain, which was to benefit from new liquidities derived from the expropriation of Spanish Jews.

The military rivalry between European states also gave them a decisive and much more direct advantage when they exported their power overseas toward the East and West Indies. Their armies, well equipped and very professional, could crush without difficulty those they encountered along the way.[24] Strong in its military superiority, and with a reserve of ideas springing from the scientific revolution, the West could now conquer the world.

3

Malthus' Law

The Agricultural Constraint

Despite its new technological dynamism, Europe constantly ran up against an obstacle recurring from the distant past: food crises. The prosperity of the eleventh, twelfth, and thirteenth centuries was rapidly broken by the return of famine at the start of the fourteenth century. Famine, plague, and war were the three scourges that struck people in various combinations. At the end of the fourteenth century, these scourges had reduced the population by more than one-third since the start of that century. The previous population maximum would not be matched until the start of the seventeenth century. This rupture would cause the crumbling of feudalism, as we have seen. The fall in population made humans suddenly scarce in relation to land. Serfs fled their lords' domains, assured of finding hospitality elsewhere.

The Renaissance corresponded to a period (around the middle of the fifteenth century) when the reduced population was liberated from the sustenance constraint. Thanks to a lower population, Europeans could profit from better agricultural production and could concentrate on the most fertile land. This process freed a portion of the population to migrate to the cities and to participate in the revival of commerce.

The same causes producing the same effects, the agricultural constraint locked in again as soon as Europe's population returned (around the middle of the seventeenth century) to the level it had reached at the start of the fourteenth century. The infernal trio of famine, plague, and war again ravaged Europe. The Thirty Years War (1618–1648) introduced dysentery, typhus, smallpox, and the plague. Famine hit France regularly between 1628 and 1638, and again from 1646 to 1652. In 1693–94 it was so severe that it was called the Great Famine. At the dawn of the eighteenth century, France was once again a poor country. How such a thing was possible after so many splendors was a paradox that economists would try to resolve.

The law of Reverend Thomas Malthus

Classical political economy, which continues to inspire economists today, was born at the end of the eighteenth century in the context of lively controversies about whether wealth came from land or from people.[25] Adam Smith and David Ricardo were the grand masters of the subject, but the most biting vision of human history—a vision to which everyone adhered—came from Thomas Malthus, a Christian minister. Malthus' Law would long determine economists' understanding of the world.

Malthus' Law can be summarized as follows: Whatever the progress achieved by human civilizations in the realms of art or technology, the income of a nation's inhabitants cannot progress. The reason is extremely simple. When the revenue of a nation tends to increase, the population tends to increase even faster. In the words of Richard Cantillon, humans, if they were not subject to the constraint of feeding themselves, would reproduce "like mice in a barn."[26] Any improvement in the standard of living would unleash exponential population growth, which would eventually be broken by a lack of available land.

Malthus' Law might appear extravagant. How is it possible for revenue to stagnate in the course of thousands and thousands of years of human existence? Yet this stagnation is confirmed by recent quantitative research on the economy. Gregory Clark makes daring comparisons in his book *Farewell to Alms: A Brief Economic History of the World*. He shows that the daily wage in ancient Babylon (1880–1600 BCE) was equivalent to 15 pounds of wheat. In Athens it rose to 26 pounds. In England in 1780, it fell back to 13 pounds. The caloric consumption of an inhabitant of Europe had certainly improved, thanks to the importing of new products (including spices, sugar, tea, and coffee from Asia and potatoes and tomatoes from America). But these additions to the diet remained minor in comparison with the monotonous consumption of bread, relieved by some modest supplements of beef, mutton, and cheese.

Comparing British agriculture (among the most productive in Europe in the eighteenth century) with agriculture in less developed societies, Clark gets astonishing results. One English peasant produced about 2,600 calories (of wheat, meat, and fat) per hour. Many so-called primitive societies do much better; the Kaulus in Indonesia produce 4,500 calories, the Mekranotis in Brazil 17,600. In view of the fact that hunter-gatherers work only a few hours a week, a formidable degradation in the human condition occurred in the course of the few tens of thousand of years that separate the discovery of agriculture from the industrial era.[27]

The law of diminishing returns

A simple principle emerges that enables us to understand these evolutions. Agricultural production is subject to a law of diminishing returns. The more you must cultivate land to nourish an expanding population, the more you must shift agricultural production to less fertile land, and the more difficult it becomes to nourish humans and their livestock. Inevitably there comes a point at which the population cannot continue to grow.

This explains the appearance of property income. In obliging people to clear and cultivate poor land, the augmentation of population offered rent to the owners of better ground, who could, without fear of competition, make its use cost more. This theory contradicts the idea developed in the eighteenth century by the Physiocrats. Led by François Quesnay, a court physician, these writers thought that by planting a fruit tree one could produce five more trees and thus nourish five times as many people as before. Land was the sole source of wealth, by this reasoning, because it inherited divine generosity. In Malthus' reasoning, the contrary was true. If God were infinitely generous, good land would be infinitely abundant and property income would be nil. Thus rent measured divine avarice, not divine generosity.

The theory of property income also explained the historical equivalence between aristocracy and wealth. The first nobles appropriated control over the best land, which procured them status and wealth. Then new arrivals acquired the last available land, taking their place in the long line of *nouveaux riches*. Schiavone concluded that in antiquity the economic foreground already was occupied by a single figure: the rent-collecting landowner. Any other image of wealth indicated only a "transitory and ambiguous" state. These were the terms that counted in all eras and all civilizations, at least until the Industrial Revolution.

THE DISMAL SCIENCE

Malthus' Law earned economics the epithet "the dismal science." For Enlightenment thinkers such as Condorcet, poverty and misery did not result from "bad" human nature; they resulted from bad government. Malthus, whose father was an admirer of the Enlightenment, wanted to show exactly the opposite: that good government eventually harmed the public good. Peace, stability, and public hygiene were transformed into curses, since all virtues favored demographic expansion and, ultimately, misery. In contrast, vices—war, violence, bad living—all created the inverse situation. They stopped demographic expansion, thereby allowing those who survived to live better. For example, the Great Plague that hit Europe in the middle of the fourteenth century improved the economic situation of the survivors.[28]

In the pre-industrial world, high mortality had a good effect. It meant many fewer mouths to feed. And bad hygiene wasn't harmful from a social point of view. When the Globe Theater opened

---

in 1599 to give performances of Shakespeare's plays, a single water closet was put at the disposal of the 500 spectators that the theater could hold. Some had to relieve themselves in the adjacent garden, if not in the theater itself, on the stairs, or in the corridors. The Court at Versailles also was known for its frightful odor.[29]

We may be astonished that any theory should proclaim equivalence between the standard of living under the reign of the great kings of the seventeenth century and the primitive life of Australian or Amazonian aboriginal peoples. How can we compare the splendors of Versailles and life to the camps of the hunter-gatherers? The answer relates to the gap between the average and the extremes. The mass of inhabitants did not live better in eighteenth-century Europe than in the African savannah several thousand years earlier. But the few rich persons were very much richer. The central paradox that summarizes all the others is that in a Malthusian world inequalities are a good thing. They do not change anything about the standard of living of the popular classes, but they raise the income of the upper class. The average income rises with inequalities. Thus inequalities increase the average income. This is indeed the reign of the prosperity of vice.[30]

Another paradox of societies governed by Malthus' Law is that work doesn't pay. The more industrious a society, the more the return per hour worked must fall. Hunter-gatherers earned as much as English workers in the earliest industries, but by working very little. A worker at the start of the nineteenth century worked 10 hours a day, more than 300 days a year on average, for the same net income. In contrast, the Huis, a society of hunter-gatherers in Venezuela whose customs and uses can be measured, work on average 2 hours a day.

Malthus' Law deeply influenced classical economists, who adhered to its pessimistic vision of human history as fated to perpetual poverty. Its worthy heir was Marx, whose work as a whole was designed to prove that the proletariat could never get rich within capitalism. The theory of Malthus also played another important role of a philosophical kind. In effect, it showed that a human being suffers under a law imposed on him that he doesn't understand. Darwin was right when he dedicated *On the Origin of Species* to Malthus.[31]

The first European country to really engage in what was called the "demographic transition" was France. This transition is the process that makes the number of children fall from the high levels of the pre-industrial era (up to ten children per woman on average) to birth rates that are associated with the modern world, meaning no more than two children on average. Economists explain that the demographic transition results from material prosperity and from advances in public health. Thanks to these factors, families shift, according to Gary Becker's expression, from the reign of quantity to that of quality. Once they are confident that their children will not die young, people have fewer children and take better care of them.

However, France invalidates this argument. Starting in the middle of the eighteenth century, even before the progress of material civilization made itself felt, the French people registered a spectacular decrease in their birth rate. In the case of France, cultural shifts were ahead of the economic ones. For example, there were more French people than Russians at the start of the eighteenth century, and four times as many French people as Britons. Had France experienced as much demographic growth as England through the nineteenth century, today there would be nearly 200 million French people in Europe.[32] These figures show the strength of the demographic forces that are in play.

Germany maintained strong demography even longer than England, passing France in the middle of the nineteenth century. Population growth is one of the major reasons why countries belatedly coming into modernity try to outstrip the others. The increasing disequilibrium between France and Germany played a role in unleashing the wars of the twentieth century.

4

UNBOUND PROMETHEUS

THE INDUSTRIAL REVOLUTION

Around the middle of the eighteenth century, Europe took an important turn, one comparable only to the Neolithic revolution. Upsetting human lives in proportions impossible to imagine a few decades earlier, the Industrial Revolution would gradually, over the course of a century, interrupt the reign of Malthus' Law. What happened?

As its name indicates, this rupture was carried along by the emergence of new industrial technologies. The most famous of them was the steam engine of James Watt. It culminated a set of innovations initially aimed at improving the pumping of water from mines, but the world would learn to do many other things with it. Poised for development were the textile industry, the railroads, and the steamship. Thanks to the steam engine, the mechanization of the world could truly begin.[33]

Aristotle explained slavery through the famous idea that industry would need no workers if a shuttle could run by itself. And if each tool could execute its specific task by itself, neither slaves nor artisans would be needed. The history of English textile weaving makes it possible to follow the outcome of this prediction very precisely.

In 1733, a clever weaver named John Kay invented what Aristotle had dreamed of: the flying shuttle. Automatic return of the shuttle made it possible to weave widths of cloth greater than the length of the weaver's arm. Thanks to Kay's invention, the speed of weaving doubled. Kay was immediately chased out of Colchester (his home town), then was pursued from town to town by rioters who understood very well that the shuttle would take "their" jobs. Kay died, destitute, in France. However, his discovery would give textile weaving in England an advantage that would last nearly 100 years, by itself accounting for England's nearly 50 percent increase in growth in the first half of the nineteenth century. The sequence of events is perfectly exemplary of how capitalism functions. Kay's machine reduced costs spectacularly. But the expansion of weaving demanded that spinning follow the same cadence. The old spinning wheels were too slow. Delays in delivery of thread increased, as did prices. It was not until 1764 that another inspired inventor, Richard Arkwright, refined a spinning machine, the water-frame, that used hydraulic energy to operate eight, then sixteen, then sixty spindles at a time. In 1777, seeking to improve the motor force of the tasks, Arkwright called on James Watt, whose steam engine would be perfected for this purpose.[34]

In the course of further development, the textile industry encountered new impediments having to do with bleaching. In the past, cloth had been whitened with curdled milk and then laid out to dry in the sun. That required a lot of meadows and a lot of cows. The chemical industry set out to solve the problem, and soon there were some radical innovations. First the textile industry switched from cow's milk to soda. But the soda came from a rare plant, the salt-wort, that was in short supply during the years of the Revolution and the Empire. Gradually, a process developed by the Frenchman Nicolas Leblanc was adopted. Chlorine, first isolated in 1774, came to be used for whitening.

The first synthetic dye, commercialized in 1856, was made by the British chemist W. H. Perkin. A mauve dress that Queen Victoria wore to the Universal Exhibition of 1862 aroused the envy of European chemists. The German industry was born of this challenge. In 1869 it synthesized alizarin, which then was substituted for the madder-rose (cultivated in Provence) as a basis for red dyes. Thanks to the exceptional profits that flowed from this development, increased research efforts combined theoretical research and the search for profit for the first time. And then the synthesis of indigo, which would be commercialized in 1901, was achieved. Along the way, in 1899, German chemists would invent aspirin, which would give rise to the modern pharmaceutical industry.[35]

The logic of industrial innovations is always the same. The race for growth pulls the backward sectors forward until the point of rupture is reached, provoking innovations that break the previous equilibrium and sometimes take an autonomous course. The dynamic is regular. One imbalance chases another, but the race ultimately results in growth in all sectors.

England, uniquely, enjoyed growth in the textile industry and in metallurgy, then in mechanical construction, and then in naval construction, all relying on exports to find outlets. England also went farther than other countries in the regionalization of activities: cotton in Manchester, mechanical construction in Glasgow, and so on. England provided the matrix for what would become, much later, the Asiatic model: an export-led growth model. On the continent, especially in France, the evolution was slower. The turn to machines progressed gradually, with production remaining artisanal longer. A century later, though, the result was the same. Industrial society had replaced rural society.

Science rediscovered

David Landes analyzed the Industrial Revolution in his book *The Unbound Prometheus* (Cambridge University Press, 1969; second edition 2003). As Landes tells it, Prometheus brought fire to humans and was nailed to a cliff by Zeus; James Watt released him, and the creative energy of humans was once again liberated. The role played by science in the process, which seems evident today, was long neglected by historians as a factor in the Industrial Revolution. It was customary to characterize the great inventions of the eighteenth century—in metallurgy, in textiles, in energy— as the work of inspired technicians and not of scholars. However, even though the talented artisans who invented the steam engine and the weaving machine lacked education in science, they could turn to scholars or their writings when that was necessary. As Joel Mokyr has shown, artisans lived in a milieu full of concern for scientific experimentation.[36] For example, when William Cooke (an English anatomist-entrepreneur who had been inspired by a lecture given by a German scholar) began to conceive the telegraph, he consulted James Faraday and then Charles Wheatstone.

Steam engines testify to the subtle interaction between artisanal innovation and scientific research. Early on, the ingenuity, mechanical intuitions, and good experimental methods of Newcomen and Papin were excellent substitutes for formal scientific training. The interaction between ingenuity and experimentation is what enabled James Watt to transform a clumsy invention into a universal source of energy. The theory of the steam engine and the way to make it more efficient came just afterward, with the work of the French physicist Sadi Carnot in 1824. Carnot showed that the temperature differential was a source of efficiency. In the next step, the English brewer-physicist James Prescott Joule established the conversion between energy and heat. The separate efforts of Joule and of Carnot were reconciled by the German physicist Rudolf Clausius, who introduced the concept of entropy. In 1850 a new science was born; it was named *thermodynamics* by an Englishman, William Thomson (later Lord Kelvin). In 1859, William Rankine's *Manual of the Steam Engine* popularized the results of thermodynamics for engineers.[37]

Mokyr summarizes the situation well when he says that, rather than ask what were the immediate causes of the Industrial Revolution, we should ask why the resultant growth wasn't interrupted by about 1850. The scientific basis had become crucial. It was not so much the miraculous "gadgets" of the great inventing years between 1760 and 1790 that counted; more important was the dynamic of scientific progress that made it possible to surmount impediments to growth.

It is useful to emphasize here that science developed more in France and in Germany than in England. England, home of the first

---

Industrial Revolution, would gradually lose its ascendancy over the industrial world. One of the reasons Mokyr cites is worth contemplating. England did not know how to adapt its education system. Its elites would continue to attend elite universities, where they learned the art of social codes. In France and Germany, the great engineering schools, created to catch up with England, would furnish the personnel of the second Industrial Revolution, that of electricity and the internal-combustion engine.

Coal, Wheat, and Slaves

In perfect conformity with the Malthusian prediction, England experienced a formidable demographic spurt in the eighteenth and nineteenth centuries,. Its population increased from 7 million in 1701 to 8.5 million in 1801, and to 15 million in 1841. The demographic explosion obeyed the traditional schema. During this period, the average age of marriage for women decreased from 26 years to 23. Not until the end of the nineteenth century was the English demographic transition, which saw the number of children decrease to the "modern" levels of two or three per woman, completed. What happened in the meantime?

To the general surprise of Malthusian economists, the doubling of the population wasn't accompanied by a loss of income. In fact, the revenue per inhabitant increased by nearly 10 percent, which proves that somehow the food problem had been resolved. How did England manage to feed all those people? New technologies would lag in finding useful applications in the agricultural sector.[38] Not until the last third of the nineteenth century would the refinement of effective synthetic fertilizers increase agricultural productivity.

So it wasn't better use of its land that allowed England to feed itself. How did England manage? The answer is simple. It exported industrial products and imported agricultural products. England adopted the model that would be used by new industrial countries in the 1970s and by China today: a strategy of growth drawn entirely from exports (and singularly in a first phase by the textile industry), profits from which made it possible to import the agricultural products that were lacking.[39]

Exports of industrial goods thus represented (as of 1830) half of England's industrial production. Never had the domestic market been able to offer outlets sufficient for national production, and never had the land available in England been sufficient to feed its people or to procure the raw materials that industry needed. Therefore, England would rely on Canada for wood, on Australia for wool, on India for jute, and on West Africa for palm oil.

England's other great reservoir of natural resources was the United States. However, exploitation of the virgin lands of the New World would run up against a problem. The fact that those lands were abundant also signified that they were scarcely populated. Manpower was rare and thus dear. Who would cultivate these new lands? The answer is sinister in our memory. Africa would supply the manpower. In "triangular trade," which began in the seventeenth century, England sold cloth to Africa, which exported slaves to America, which exported its raw cotton to England. The American economic historians William Fogel and Stanley Engerman overturned historiography on this subject with their 1974 book *Time on the Cross*, in which they showed how effective the system was. According to some calculations, slaves produced two-thirds of the American exports destined for England, principally sugar and cotton. If the lack of slaves signaled the decline of the Roman Empire, it was the abundance of African slaves that would enable the rise of the British Empire

Besides the natural resources it could import, England was also profiting from an inestimable domestic resource: coal. This offered an unexpected alternative to the traditional energy sources, all of which depended, directly or indirectly, on available land, on arable land to feed people and animals, or on forests for energy from timber. England was beginning to lack forests and thus was fortunate to possess abundant coal. Coal would become the main source of energy for the textile factories. But it was also the fuel for the railways and the steamships that connected England to its markets and its suppliers.

The loop was complete. The "Promethean" miracle traced a loop around British coal reserves, American land, and African slaves. Malthus' Law was vanquished, but ingloriously.

5

Perpetual Growth

Smith, Marx, and Humanoids

Around the middle of the eighteenth century, economists were thinking about the possibility of an economy entirely governed by the functioning of markets.[40] The author who set the terms in which people still think about the market economy was the Scottish economist Adam Smith, who expounded his theories in *An Inquiry into the Causes of the Wealth of Nations*, published in 1776.

Smith wanted to show that, thanks to the market, each person could specialize in a job, such as that of a doctor, a lawyer, a baker, or a cobbler, without having to worry about lacking merchandise that he didn't make himself. This silent cooperation, this "invisible hand" that links all participants in exchanges, relied on an idea that inspired this famous sentence: "It is not from the benevolence of the butcher, the brewer, or the baker, that we expect our dinner, but from their regard to their own interest." Here Smith is a philosopher as much as an economist. The word "interest" as Smith uses it doesn't have the neutral significance that it later acquired to characterize economic calculation. As Albert Hirschman (himself an economist and a philosopher) brilliantly showed in his 1997 book *The Passions and the Interests*, it is a term that was long synonymous with cupidity or greed, figuring in Dante's *Inferno* alongside pride and envy.[41] In *The Theory of Moral Sentiments* (a book published before *The Wealth of Nations*), Smith showed that he had no illusions about interest: "For to what purpose is all the toil and bustle of this world? What is the end of avarice and ambition, of the pursuit of wealth, of power, and preeminence? . . . From whence, then, arises that emulation which runs through all the different ranks of men, and what are the advantages which we propose by that great purpose of human life which we call bettering our condition?" The answer proposed by Smith is what one might call the desire of being desired: "To be observed, to be attended to, to be taken notice of with sympathy, complacency, and approbation, are all the advantages which we can propose to derive from [emulation]. It is the vanity, not the ease, or the pleasure, which interests us."

However, what distinguishes greed from other passions relates to an essential difference. Well directed, greed can contribute to the public good, whereas other passions are destructive. The author who inspired Smith was Bernard Mandeville, who in 1705 had published *A Fable of the Bees*, subtitled *Private Vices, Public Virtues*. The poetic conclusion sums up the moral:

> So Vice is beneficial found,
> When it's by Justice lop't and bound,
> Nay, where the People would be just,

As necessary to the State
As hunger is to make 'em eat.
Bare virtue can't make Nations live
In splendor. . . .

By showing that ambition, vanity, and need for consideration can be assuaged by an improvement in material conditions, Smith could enunciate his theory of the "invisible hand": "Without any intervention of law, therefore, the private interests and passions of men naturally lead them to divide and distribute the stock of every society among all the different employments carried on in it as nearly as possible in the proportion which is most agreeable to the interest of the whole society."

Hence it is not useful to ask about the moral motives that lead people to want to get rich; it suffices to concentrate on their consequences. The market is content to measure the effort that each person is disposed to expend to enrich himself. This is the true message of Adam Smith. In a famous example, he explains that in a society of hunters the price of a beaver can be compared with that of a deer by forming a ratio between the time necessary to kill each. If it takes twice as long to kill a deer, its price will necessarily be twice the price of the beaver. If it were worth less, hunters would immediately stop hunting deer. The same reasoning would apply to beavers in the inverse case. One need not know the motivations of these categories of hunters to reach this result.

In a more elaborated form, the market does more than that. Thanks to the division of labor it encourages, it enables workers to be more productive. Smith remarks in his famous discussion of the manufacture of pins (inspired by a trip to Normandy that he made as tutor to a young aristocrat) that ten workers manage to produce 48,000 pins each day, whereas one worker left to himself would manage to produce 200 at most. By centralizing the production of pins, one can multiply the productivity of each worker by 20 or 30. What limits this process, Smith explains, is the size of the market. Though it is excellent to divide up tasks, one must find people to whom to sell the 48,000 pins produced. If the demand is for no more than 200 pins per day, only one worker will have to be employed, even if that worker's productivity is lower. Still, as wealth increases, one can conceive that an endogenous process of increasing productivity will take effect. The more society enriches itself, the more the division of labor increases, the more productivity increases, and the stronger the growth becomes. Infinite enrichment becomes possible.

Adam Smith himself did not go farther than to say that the example of the pin factory led him to desire that the market sphere be as large as it could be. He called for the liquidation of non-commercial activities (domestic activities) and expressed the wish that the greatest number of activities go through the market. And, as the catchword says, everybody would win—those who buy and those who sell.

Capital

Let us now consider another point of view. "That boy of mine," says a woman whose testimony Karl Marx reports, "when he was 7 years old I used to carry him on my back to and fro through the snow, and he used to have to work 16 hours a day. . . . I have often knelt down to feed him as he stood by the machine, for he could not leave it or stop."[42] Marx, who published his masterwork *Capital* a century after Adam Smith, had before his eyes the transformation of British society induced by capitalism. For him the market was not a factor of universal enrichment but rather of exploitation of some people by others. It did not pacify society; instead it fueled an internal war: the struggle between classes.

Thanks to Marx, the condition of the working class entered into economics books. Industrial work was no longer an abstract principle, "an idea for the future"; it had become a miserable reality. To grasp the way in which capital exploited work, Marx introduced a basic opposition between "labor" and "the force of labor." In order to grasp the meaning of this distinction, let us suppose that a beaver hunter spends 10 hours killing one animal. The price of that beaver then will be, as Smith says, the monetary equivalent of 10 hours of work. The snag is that nothing guarantees that the hunter will be paid that amount. If he is hired by a capitalist, how much should the employer pay him? The market price of the hunter corresponds, at a minimum, to the cost of feeding, clothing, and housing him—in short, the cost of enabling him to work. This is the price of his "force of labor." Should he be paid more? Not if there are a sufficient number of workers ready to accept this task in order to avoid dying of hunger. In that case, it suffices to pay him the minimum wage. Let us say that it takes the equivalent of 4 hours of work to feed a worker, and that he can work 10 hours. The difference corresponds to the "added value" that the boss could pocket. This *surplus value* is the source of profit. Like the generous gods in Physiocratic thinking, Nature allows capitalists to get rich by using the unique capacity of people to work more than it would cost simply to live.

Marx was therefore convinced that capitalism could generate profits only on the condition of maintaining the proletariat in a state of want. "Whatever the rate of salaries, the condition of the worker must get worse as capital accumulates. [The bourgeoisie] is incapable of ensuring the existence of its slave even within his slavery." Malthus made demographic pressure the main reason for this dismal equilibrium. Marx imported Malthusian theory into the industrial world by means of a new idea: the industrial reserve army. To impose low salaries, sources of surplus value, capitalism needs to maintain a mass of proletarians without jobs, which obliges those who do have jobs to accept a subsistence salary. Instead of demographic pressure, capitalism substitutes a poverty constructed by itself for the purpose of its smooth functioning.

Humanoids

Marx thought, as did Aristotle and the English political economist David Ricardo, that machines were competing with workers. For him, new machines reduced the demand for labor, which allowed an increase in the reserve army and condemned the proletariat to eternal poverty. The paradox is that a machine allows the work of the person who operates it to be more productive, making it possible to raise the worker's salary. This was the foundation of what would be called neoclassical theory, which adapted the theories of Smith and Ricardo to the new realities of the industrial world.[43] According to it, man and machine are complementary, as man and the land could have been in pre-industrial time. Profit is not theft; it measures the contribution of machines to the productivity of labor.[44]

The major difference between land and capital is that when the working population increases, the number of machines can also be increased, whereas it is difficult (sometimes impossible) to increase the amount of cultivated land. Therefore, in an industrial society, demography is no longer a problem. Per capita income can remain stable despite a rise in population. Industry foils the law of diminishing returns. The scale of productivity has no effect on efficiency. If one doubles the number of workers and also doubles the number of machines, then one can safely double production. Unlike agriculture, industry obeys a law of *constant returns*.

Yet could income per capita be not merely stable but indefinitely growing? Increasing the number of machines could not be the solution; a person has only one head and two arms. There must be a point at which increasing the number of machines operated by a worker becomes useless. We owe to the economist Robert Solow the simple and powerful theory that takes account of this missing link.[45] To the two factors of production—capital and labor—Solow adds a third, which he calls "technical progress." John Kay did not put two old machines in the hands of the weaver, but an entirely new machine that enabled him to operate several spindles. Today, by pressing a single button, one can perform a cascade of tasks that would formerly have been done by several persons—for example, dictating, typing, and sending a letter.

Technical progress enables a single worker to have "several pairs of arms." It operates like a multiplier of the number of hours worked. Thanks to new technologies, a task that in the nineteenth century required four hours of work could be done in only one hour in the twentieth century. Underneath the apparent work of a single person, several "humanoids" are silently working on that person's account. Hence per capita income can now increase at the same rate as technical progress, which measures the demographics of humanoids.

Everything seems clear, except the answer to this question: Where does technical progress come from?

Mozart and Schumpeter

To grasp the import of the world opened by the Industrial Revolution, and to compare it with what preceded it, the economist Michael Kremer has proposed an ambitious theory that links the Malthusian theory of the pre-industrial era and the theory of modern growth.[46] Kremer presupposes that before the industrial era the production of ideas resulted from a simple law that we can call "the Mozart principle." Each person has an equal chance of having a great idea, of being a potential Mozart. This reasonable hypothesis implements an extremely powerful process. The more human beings there are, the more ideas they have, and the more these ideas enable the invention of new techniques, which in turn push back the economic (and hence demographic) limits of the societies in which they develop. New humans can thus be born, their ideas can flourish, and the process continues *ad infinitum*.

An autocatalytic mechanism goes to work, which explains why the human population has grown so rapidly. There were 10 million humans in the Neolithic, 200 million in the time of Jesus, and a billion at the start of the industrial age in 1800. Each person tends, on average, to bring a solution to the problem posed by his own existence.

Can we understand the sources of technical progress in the same terms in the new industrial world that opened at the end of the eighteenth century? Not completely. In the framework of modern growth, an autocatalytic phenomenon is also at work, but it is the size of the markets rather than demographic growth that explains its dynamic. Adam Smith had already noted in the example of the pin factory that the growth of the market sphere encourages economies of scale that make workers productive. Theoreticians of endogenous growth, especially Paul Romer and Robert Lucas, would take up this intuition.[47] The essential idea is *increasing returns to scale*. The more markets develop, the more worthwhile innovation becomes. In effect, an inventor can recuperate his investment all the more easily when a large number of consumers are reached. It is no longer the population that rules growth, but wealth that feeds itself.

In the two centuries that followed the publication of *The Wealth of Nations*, economists turned away from the idea of increasing returns to scale. The reason for that choice is found in the work of Adam Smith himself. While he was emphasizing the beneficial effects of the division of labor, Smith also wanted to demonstrate that *competition* among producers allows a balance to be achieved that is both just and effective—that of the market. This is the thesis of the invisible hand.

Economists would quickly realize that Smith's proposition about the benefits of increasing returns to scale and his proposition about the benefits of competition were contradictory. As the example of the pin factory demonstrates, the big owner has an advantage over the small one. Profiting from economies of scale allows him to divide up tasks within his business, and he can sell things cheaper and so make smaller businesses disappear. Thus, as Marx also intuited, this reasoning leads to forecasting a greater and greater concentration of production, which will fatally, sooner or later, thwart pure and perfect competition. Thus the principle of increasing returns to scale, pushed to its extreme, contradicts the laws of competition. It leads to a theory of monopolies.

***

The difficulty is resolved, however, if one manages to conceive what might appear to be a contradiction in terms: monopolistic competition. Outlined before World War II but overshadowed by the rise of Keynesian theory, it owes its revival to the approaches inspired by Joseph Schumpeter, an economist of Austrian origin who became a professor at Harvard University.[48] Schumpeter's argument can be summarized as follows: Monopolies are ephemeral. As soon as a firm has achieved monopoly over a product, other firms will try to take it away by inventing products that will make obsolete those that were in the hands of the first monopoly. According to this Schumpeterian vision, which is dominant among present-day economists, capitalism escapes the categories of both Adam Smith and Karl Marx. Contrary to Smith's view, it is not a sign of solidarity that the cobbler and the baker each offer the other what he needs; instead there is a blind rivalry between the bakers who use modern techniques and those who delay doing so. And, contrary to Marx's view, this is not a sign of the pauperization of the working class, either, for technical progress makes the worker more productive and enables him to be paid more.

Technical progress is not the worker's friendly helper, however. The worker is no longer the slave of a master, as in ancient times, but he doesn't become the master of the brave humanoids who are working freely for him, as Solow suggested. The worker in the modern world is the slave of a new uncertainty that looms over his fate. Technical progress is both creative and destructive, and the boundary is quickly crossed. Everything is fine so long as growth is strong enough to bind the wounds it constantly opens in the body social. But when it slows—or, worse, when it becomes negative as the result of a major disruption—the equilibrium can be shattered.

II

Prosperity and Depression

6

THE ECONOMIC CONSEQUENCES OF THE WAR

THE ECONOMIC CONSEQUENCES OF THE PEACE

In *The Economic Consequences of the Peace*, published in 1919, a young British economist, John Maynard Keynes, took the reader into a moribund Paris. Europe had been stripped bare, four empires had fallen, and the center of the world was shifting to the United States. In this ambiance of dust and blood, one old man felt "about France what Pericles felt of Athens—unique value in her, nothing else mattering; but his theory of politics was Bismarck's. He had one illusion—France; and one disillusion—mankind, including Frenchmen, and his colleagues not least."

French Prime Minister Georges Clemenceau, a figure emblematic of the past, would sign the Treaty of Versailles, which ratified Germany's defeat. Clemenceau wanted to break the German dynamo once and for all. He wanted to ensure that Germany would never again outstrip France. Between the creation of the Reich in

1871 and the start of World War I, Germany's industrial production had increased fivefold. Its economic dynamism could be seen on all fronts. It was already at the heels of England in world commerce, with a particularly strong position in such expanding modern industries as chemicals, machinery, and electrical energy. German agriculture also enjoyed a favorable conjuncture. Germany was a pioneer in agricultural modernization, in the use of fertilizer and in mechanization, and in sophisticated crop rotation.[1]

Germans observed the demographic collapse of France with schadenfreude. In 1870 the two nations had possessed almost comparable wealth, but by 1914 Germany was ahead by more than 70 percent. German ambitions were fed by this new economic superiority. The German historian Heinrich Winkler summed up the situation: "The German economy was not far from overtaking that of Britain, the motherland of the Industrial Revolution and of imperialism. . . . The German Reich was among the world's great economic powerhouses, perhaps the greatest of them all. Yet all this was not enough for the political right. It was not enough that Germany should remain a mere 'great power': it had to become the leading power of the world."[2]

These were the ambitions that Clemenceau wanted to check. And to do so he obtained the punitive provisions in the Treaty of Versailles: Germany had to cede nearly all of its merchant marine and give the Allies control over three rivers: the Oder, the Rhine, and the Danube. It had to abandon its loans and financial credits in its overseas possessions, with the Allies keeping the right to expropriate any new credits by German residents abroad as war reparations. The Treaty of Versailles also stipulated that the vanquished nation should give to France all rights pertaining to exports from mines in the Saar, that after an election upper Silesia should be given to Poland, and that Germany should pay France for all lost revenue on its own mines calculated on their prewar profit rates. Moreover, Germany should give 25 million tons of coal to the Allies each year for a period of 10 years. Finally, it had to grant all of them the status of most favored nation.

When it had fulfilled these provisions, Germany would have paid the equivalent of a million pounds sterling by May 1, 1921— and the Allies could choose any guarantee they thought necessary. But to this first million pounds were to be added four others, which would then be completed by a sum considered sufficient compensation to civilians for losses suffered during the war. The Treaty of Versailles did not define a total sum or any schedule for the reparations. As a comparison, Keynes estimated that a similar indemnity paid by France to Bismarck for the 1870 war would have corresponded to 500 million pounds.

The very outrageousness of the treaty made it practically impossible to enforce. Despite the invasion of the Ruhr in 1923 by France and Belgium to obtain their due, the amount paid by Germany would remain insignificant. But the wound inflicted on Germany by this extreme treaty was deep, especially because, despite the 1918 armistice, there was still hope of a "rightful peace." Those who were persuaded that there was no basic antagonism between Germany and the United States put all their hope in President Woodrow Wilson's efforts to obtain a moderate peace settlement. But since Wilson had to bend to harsh French demands, Germany would long harbor the idea of a "knife in the back" that would fuel the resentment from which Nazism was born after the crisis of 1929.

THE REPUBLIC DIES

The Weimar Republic was established in November of 1918. Its founders wanted to create the most democratic system possible by means of universal suffrage, with popular election of the Reichstag assembly and of the president of the republic, and also with a referendum procedure by which the government's power could be challenged at any moment. Moreover, the republic's founders adopted proportional representation, which sacrificed concern for political efficiency to democratic accountability.

In hindsight, it is easy to explain the failure of the Weimar Republic by the circumstances of its birth. Tainted by defeat in war, the government had a hard time establishing its legitimacy. On the right, nationalist circles denounced it as non-German, as born of the scandal of Versailles. On the left, the bloody confrontations of 1919–20, in the course of which two revolutionary leaders (Karl Liebknecht and Rosa Luxemburg) would be assassinated, left indelible traces.

Yet Christian Baechler argues forcefully that "while the conditions of birth and development of the Weimar democracy were indeed difficult, at the outset democracy itself was not to blame." "Even by January 1933," he continues, "Hitler's accession to power was not inevitable. Other alternatives were available to Germany."[3]

A divided society

The postwar period reopened the wounds that the prewar years of strong growth had created. Between 1870 and 1913, Germany's urbanization had been massive and brutal.[4] In Baechler's words: "The great city with its agitation and its individualism aroused nostalgia for a return to nature and to the healthy and simple life of the countryside, and even worry about decadent morality. The diversification of society in the large cities offered possibilities for social ascension, but it also invited the risk of social decline and a feeling of insecurity. Many turned to the State as the protector of last resort."[5]

German society, despite the new geographic and social mobility, remained fragmented, rigid, and more marked by differences in status than other Western societies. Alongside distinctions between the bourgeois and working classes, between salaried workers and artisans, there persisted premodern criteria of a feudal kind. The nobility kept a privileged position, as it did in other countries of Western Europe on the eve of the war. But in Germany it had a much more important political and social role. The Junkers, the great landowners east of the Elba, enjoyed specifically feudal privileges over their domains, including rights to police and to appoint church and school personnel. The nobility remained closely tied to the military monarchy and to the bureaucracy, and thus held a strategic place in the power system. All the German chancellors until the war had been nobles, as had most secretaries of state of the empire and most ministers of Prussia and Saxony.[6]

Prussian bureaucratic and military power permeated the whole society. In Germany the state was "an end in itself and the incarnation of Reason" typified in Hegel's philosophy or Max Weber's sociology. Bureaucracy was supposed to represent "the common good faced with the chaos of contradictory interests of the market," which did not favor the establishment of parliamentary government.

In addition, there was a religious division in German society. One-third of the population was Catholic, and that third was the political base of the Deutsche Zentrumspartei (German Center Party). The Protestant churches were very linked to the state, but German Protestantism was now more a rigorous morality than a faith. With the weakening of religious ties, there was a search for a substitute theology—a political faith.

Despite their tiny number (0.6 percent of the population), the Jews' participation in the socialist revolution and their political emancipation associated them with the defeat in the World War, and Hitler would be deeply affected by the thesis of their responsibility for it. Jews were contradictorily accused of favoring both capitalism and revolution, of wanting to "dominate the planet by the two forms of materialism that are capitalism and Bolshevism."

Despite its successes before the war, Germany offered a pathological version of the European model of the nation-state. The myth of the (Germanic) Roman Empire had survived longer there than in any other country. The religious schism had left deep traces. The tension between Germany and Austria had not been resolved, and the crumbling of the Austro-Hungarian Empire had revived the issue of national unity. Finally, the adoption of a real parliamentary government was achieved only after the 1918 defeat, which made it fragile.

The life and death of the Weimar Republic

Despite the difficulties of the armistice, economic recovery occurred and growth resumed.[7] Germany achieved its industrial reconstruction by 1922, and meanwhile the unemployment rate decreased to 1.5 percent. Yet everything changed dramatically in January 1923, when French and Belgian troops decided to occupy the Ruhr to force the Germans to pay their war debts. The Weimar government called for passive resistance and financed the civil service on credit. But resorting to printing money to finance public deficits triggered hyperinflation. The price index increased by a billion in six months. This ruined creditors; salaries in the private sector were affected by growing unemployment and by the lag in salary increases in relation to inflation. While artisans, businessmen, and entrepreneurs came out of the budgetary adjustment relatively well, state employees were its first victims. Senior civil servants and the intellectual bourgeoisie also suffered from a leveling of salaries.

In November 1923, after the French withdrawal, a new hope for stabilization arose. A currency in parallel to the mark, the Rentenmark, was created on November 16. Guaranteed by gold reserves, themselves secured by a mortgage on Germany's industrial and agricultural capital, this inspired confidence. Price stability was quickly recovered, and in April 1924 a new agreement concerning reparations, the Dawes Plan, was negotiated. It offered Germany stability and a manageable repayment schedule. During the two first years, the budget was not touched, which granted the country the moratorium it had so long desired.

The period 1924–1929 was the golden age of the Weimar Republic. Monetary stabilization restored the confidence of investors and enabled a flow of foreign capital, especially from the United States, to finance the relaunching of the economy.[8] In 1928, salaries were 20 percent higher than they had been in 1913. Great artists (among them Bertolt Brecht and the Bauhaus designers) produced unforgettable work. The Republic was saved.

But the crisis of 1929 upset everything. Germany was the first industrial country to be hit by the international economic crisis, and one of the two to be hit hardest. (The other was the United States.) The unemployment rate, as in the US, reached 25 percent.[9]

Starting in 1930, the popularity of extremist parties—both the Kommunistische Partei Deutschlands and the Nationale Sozialistische Deutsche Arbeiter Partei (a.k.a. Nazis)—soared. The Sozialdemokratische Partei Deutschlands, which had been the main political party during the Weimar Republic, was overtaken electorally by the Nazis in 1932. The SPD, the founding party of the Weimar government, had used all its weight to avert a revolutionary shift to Bolshevism after the war, thereby incurring the hatred of the extreme left for having liquidated the Spartacists (the movement led by Liebknecht and Luxemburg) as well as the enmity of the extreme right for having signed the armistice. The extreme right itself did not have much electoral weight before the Nazis' upsurge, but then it went from 2.6 percent of votes in May 1928 to 18.3 percent in September 1930, reaching 37.3 percent in July 1932. The Communist Party went from 10.6 percent in 1928 to 13.2 percent in 1930 and to 16.9 percent in November 1932.

It was the Protestant middle classes, especially disillusioned civil servants and pensioners, disappointed by both liberalism and conservatism, that voted for the Nazis.[10] Anti-liberal reaction at the universities reflected the decline in the status of traditional elites. Workers in large factories resisted the influence of Nazism. Contrary to what is often asserted, the unemployed contributed little to its rise. There is even a negative correlation between the unemployed and the Nazi vote, in contrast to what was observed for the Communist Party. The correlation between indebtedness among the old middle classes and peasants and the propensity to vote for the National Socialists is instead very clear. The disintegration of

German society under the influence of the 1929 crisis would bring Hitler to the chancellorship in January 1933. But nothing was written beforehand. Hitler was called to power when the circumstances were slowly improving and the Nazis might have run out of steam. As Heinrich Winkler puts it, "given the political will, the power centre around Hindenburg could have prevented Hitler's takeover of the state."[11] One trembles before the simple conclusion that there was nothing inevitable about Hitler's becoming the leader of Germany.

7

The Great Crisis and Its Lessons

1929

The crisis that began in the fall of 1929 is the blackest moment ever experienced by world capitalism—so far. Starting on Wall Street, the crisis reached Europe and then the rest of the world. The specter of 1929 continues to haunt world leaders today. During the subprime crisis of 2007, the chairman of the Federal Reserve System, Ben Bernanke, explicitly tried to avoid a recurrence. And the many resemblances between these two exceptional crises are indeed astonishing.

The Roaring Twenties

The crisis of 1929 in the United States interrupted a decade of growth known today as the Roaring Twenties. The factors producing the modern consumer society and the "American way of life" became widely diffused: the automobile, electricity, the cinema. Growth was driven by petroleum, rubber, the radio, and a construction boom.

The production of cars tripled, from 1.9 million in 1919 to 5.9 million in 1929.

On December 4, 1928, President Calvin Coolidge concluded his final speech to Congress on a triumphant note: "No Congress of the United States ever assembled, on surveying the state of the Union, has met with a more pleasing prospect than that which appears at the present time." Yet a fidgety stock market had alternated highs (in 1924) and lows (in 1926), and a speculation boom had begun in 1927. In the spring, the governors of the Banks of England, France, and Germany had come to the United States to ask the American monetary authorities to make a gesture to help the European economy, but had failed. The Federal Reserve (known informally as "the Fed") had nevertheless lowered its interest rate from 4 percent to 3.5 percent. According to Lionel Robbins, then a professor at London School of Economics, "from [the summer of 1927], according to all the evidence, the situation got completely out of control."[12] Between 1926 and 1929, stock prices doubled. The euphoria spread to small savers. A joke reported by the economist John Kenneth Galbraith testifies to the atmosphere: "The rich man's chauffeur drove with his ears laid back to catch the news of an impending move in Bethlehem Steel."[13]

Gradually, beginning in 1928, the Fed would nevertheless raise its rates to brake what Alan Greenspan would much later call the "irrational exuberance" of financial markets. By January 1929 the discount rate was already back to 5 percent. On February 14, 1929, the New York Federal Reserve Bank proposed lifting the rate from 5 percent to 6 percent to curb speculation. A long controversy followed, and the rates were not increased until the end of the summer, when they finally were raised to 6 percent. But that rate hike came too late. It has been established that the American economy was already entering the crisis at the start of the autumn of 1929.[14]

The crash

October 24 was the first of the days that history identifies with the 1929 panic. On that "Black Thursday" 12 million shares were sold, as opposed to the daily average of 4 million. Around 11:30, the market went into a panic. Eleven speculators had already committed suicide. Outside, "a mysterious roar was heard, and a crowd gathered." At midday, the greatest bankers in New York—Charles Mitchell, president of National City Bank, Albert Wiggin, president of Chase National, William Potter, president of Guaranty Trust, and Thomas Lamot, principal associate of Morgan—gathered. These grand masters of finance tried to turn back the tide by buying shares. Once the news spread, prices immediately rose. The *Times* saluted the episode: "The financial community is now secure, knowing that the most powerful banks in the country are ready to prevent panic." But on "Black Tuesday," October 29, the panic resumed, and it was now irresistible. Sixteen million shares changed hands. Prices plummeted. It was the start of a spiral leading to the abyss. On October 31 the Fed lowered the discount rate to 5 percent—in vain. The fall continued. A first trough was reached on November 13, when prices had already lost half their value. In the following three years, Wall Street would lose 85 percent of the level reached in September 1929.

Purchases of consumer durables (cars, furniture, washing machines, and so on) would be the first spring of growth to break, since consumer goods were intrinsically sensitive to economic cycles. You have to feed yourself every day, but you can put off buying a car or a washing machine. A few years earlier, consumer credit had appeared, disrupting American consumption habits. Eighty-five percent of furniture items, 80 percent of phonographs, and 75 percent of washing machines were financed on credit. At the time, a product bought on credit was seized in the event of default on repayment, without consideration of payments already made; that made consumers even more hesitant about purchases. In 1930, consumption of durable goods abruptly decreased by 20 percent, and it would decrease 50 percent between 1929 and 1933. Car purchases tumbled by two-thirds between 1929 and 1932.

The real-estate crisis was another factor in the overturning of the macroeconomic equilibrium. Construction of new housing had more than doubled in 1926 in relation to the prewar figure, and so the downturn was even more spectacular. Here, as in the market in consumer durables, credit was an aggravating factor.

Farmers were among the collateral victims of the crisis. Unlike other sectors, agriculture had not been booming. Since the end of the war, overproduction had been common, the amount of land cultivated in the United States having increased to compensate for the lowering of production in belligerent countries. With the return of peace, the excess supply depressed prices constantly. With the crisis, the net income of farmers collapsed, tumbling 70 percent between 1929 and 1933.

The financial crisis

The economist Peter Temin pinpoints the fall in consumption of durable goods in 1930 as the principal factor in the economy's downward plunge.[15] Temin can be located in the Keynesian camp of interpretations of the crisis, relying on intuitions contained in the *General Theory*. Keynes' book, published in 1936, would have a deep influence on economists and on the conduct of economic policy after the war. For Keynes, the initial contraction of activity tended to be propagated throughout the economy by a self-maintaining spiral. The fall in automobile purchases threw factory workers out of work; they then reduced their spending and thereby propagated the depression to other sectors. A "crisis multiplier" was established that only the government could eliminate.

Also much in evidence were bank failures. In their monumental *Monetary History of the United States 1867–1960*[16] Milton Friedman and Anna Schwartz challenged the Keynesian interpretation and instead privileged the role of financial factors. In Friedman's scenario, the sequence of events was as follows: The collapse of activity imperiled banks' balance sheets, which worried depositors, who, becoming distrustful (rightly or wrongly) of the most vulnerable banks, withdrew their deposits, which pushed those banks to bankruptcy. In the years 1930–1933, half of American banks disappeared owing to liquidation or absorption; there were 29,000 banks before the crisis and only 12,000 remained. Between 1929 and 1933, American monetary value (liquidity) contracted by one-third. Bank crises then deprived the most vulnerable debtors of sources for refinancing and pushed them to bankruptcy. Now those being directly affected included farmers, small businesses, and insolvent households. Research by Ben Bernanke has shown that bank failures anticipated, almost month by month, the plunge of the United States into the crisis of the 1930s.[17]

The monetary authorities failed to react. Though realizing that interest rates were very low (1–2 percent), they did not inject liquidity to save the banks. According to Friedman's interpretation, this was the main cause of the disaster: The monetary authorities of the time were not up to dealing with the crisis. They worsened it by not reacting to the collapse of the banking system. It wasn't until February 1932 that President Herbert Hoover, famous for having predicted in 1930 that recovery was "just around the corner," finally created a Reconstruction Finance Corporation and gave it public funds to be lent to financial establishments in difficulty.

The truth is no doubt situated between these two conceptions, the Keynesian and the monetarist. The crisis of 1930 is initially explained by the factors Temin emphasized: The crumbling of confidence provoked by the Wall Street collapse pulled down the morale of households, which compressed their demand and unleashed a vicious circle with respect to sales outlets. But the breadth and the scope of the depression from 1930 to 1933 were due principally to the monetary and financial factors emphasized by Friedman: The crisis in demand was transformed into a much deeper banking crisis, which could have been controlled by the central bank if it had grasped its import.

An international crisis

The 1929 crisis would never have assumed the worldwide proportions it did without the crumbling of international trade. As was the case 80 years later, the speed with which a crisis starting in the United States could reach all countries was astonishing. International commerce experienced a formidable retraction. World imports were reduced from 3 billion in April 1929 to 1 billion in February 1933. The domestic mistakes of the American authorities concerning the banks were compounded by errors in trade policy. In 1930 Congress passed the Smoot-Hawley Tariff Act, which called for a 40 percent increase on tariffs on wheat, cotton, meat, and industrial products. So the American crisis spread through international exchanges as countries affected by the American tariffs hurried to take retaliatory measures.

The economic crisis also created a crisis in raw materials that imperiled the exporting countries. In Latin America, the prices of primary materials decreased by one-third between 1929 and 1933. To free themselves from the weight of their debts, most Latin American countries went into bankruptcy. Only Argentina resisted the temptation to default on its debt repayment.

The American financial earthquake spread rapidly across Europe, exacerbated by the imbalances inherited from World War I, specifically the plans for rescheduling German debt (the Dawes Plan in 1924 and the Young Plan in 1929). Not until the Lausanne Conference of 1932 did the Allies understand the futility of wanting to "make Germany pay." Shortly after the resignation of Chancellor Heinrich Brüning in May 1932, Germany secured the financial concessions that should have been given much earlier. As we saw, that was too late. Germany, living off a perfusion of international credit, was immediately overtaken by the crisis. The absence of available financing explains in large part why budgetary policy played no role in the resolution of the crisis. (Another factor was the financial orthodoxy of the period.)

Like investors within the American banking system, international capital fled the countries that appeared vulnerable. Currencies danced crazily with each other. In May 1931, the bankruptcy of the great Austrian bank Kreditanstalt burst a dam, and the flood took down Hungarian, Czech, Romanian, Polish, and German banks.

Then it was the turn of Great Britain to be at the heart of the storm. Suddenly the gold reserves of the Bank of England seemed insufficient. On September 21, 1931, the pound was floated. The dollar was threatened in turn, inciting caution among American authorities, which explains the lack of reaction denounced by Milton Friedman. Then it was the turn of the French franc. Under the socialist-led Popular Front government (1936–1937), capital would leave France, previously considered the safest haven.

Throughout the period, monetary authorities tried to reassure investors and speculators by maintaining the convertibility of their currencies into gold as long as they could. As is emphasized by the work of Barry Eichengreen, the harmful effects of this system are clearly apparent, for as soon as a country abandoned the gold standard, growth resumed and capital flooded in. This was the case in England starting in 1931, in the United States in 1933, and in France in 1936. The paradox of this period is that the postwar trauma of high inflation made monetary authorities very worried about the idea of abandoning monetary orthodoxy, even when their economies were subject to severe deflation.

Keynes' General Theory

No government understood what really had happened in 1929. Most remained convinced that it was first necessary to reestablish confidence by maintaining a balance in public finances as well as the convertibility of their currency. But by doing so, all of them aggravated the depression. Like the doctors in Moliere's play who recommend bleeding, they would weaken and sometimes kill the patients they were trying to cure. It would take the publication of Keynes'

---

book *The General Theory of Employment, Interest and Money* (1936) to give economists a framework that enabled them to think about this new subject: the macroeconomic equilibrium.[18]

Keynes went to war against Say's Law, named after Jean-Baptiste Say, a French economist of the early nineteenth century who summarized his doctrine in this famous formula: "Offer always creates its own demand." For Say, a person sells one thing because he foresees buying another. If I sell my labor (or chickens, or automobiles), it is in order to answer a need, to feed a new demand. Therefore there is a game of feedback between supply and demand. No long-lasting imbalance can appear between these two terms.

To grasp the meaning of Keynes' critique of Say's Law, let us consider the difference between Robinson Crusoe alone on his island and a business operating in the market economy. Imagine that Crusoe finds that he doesn't have enough fishing rods. He is confronted with a simple dilemma: either continue to fish with his current rods or "invest" by making new rods. In the latter case, he knows that he will have less time to fish; he has to reduce his consumption, an act that we also call saving. For Crusoe, the act of investing and the act of saving are inseparable; he knows that he is reducing his consumption today in order to be able to increase it tomorrow.

But this concomitance is lost in a market economy. When individuals reduce their consumption and increase their savings, they wish (like Crusoe) to consume the fruits of this act later. The rational use of this saving would therefore be to invest in order to respond tomorrow to this delayed consumption. But the fisherman who today observes a reduction in the demand for fish might legitimately wonder if it will actually increase tomorrow. Should he really "profit" from the fall in sales in order to commission new fishing rods?

71

Let us suppose that he doesn't think so, that he is worried about the reduction in demand he has noticed. If he is worried, he will reduce his investment even beyond the levels that were initially foreseen. An imbalance is formed. Consumption is reduced, but so is investment. In theory, at the macroeconomic level, this imbalance should make interest rates fall, as a result of abundant saving, and incite business to invest. However, Keynes contrasted this theoretical scenario with a more mechanical one. When consumption and investment both decrease, businesses lay off workers. Impoverished by these layoffs, households consume even less. This morose climate doesn't incite businesses to invest more. The initial disequilibrium is multiplied, perhaps considerably. A new equilibrium emerges: an *equilibrium of underemployment.*

Keynes' critique of Say's Law is simple to formulate. Spending one's income presupposes that one *has* an income, but an unemployed person doesn't have one and so cannot spend. Implicitly, Say's theory presupposes that an unemployed person continues to consume. In modern terms, one would say that he continues to act as if he anticipates that his unemployment is temporary. But as soon as he adjusts his expenses to his actual income, a vicious circle appears. A lower income entails fewer expenses, which entails fewer sales outlets for businesses, which entails less hiring, and so on. This is Keynes' *multiplier effect.*

Keynes' heritage

"The morals, the politics, the literature, and the religion of the age joined in a grand conspiracy for the promotion of savings. . . . A rich man could, after all, enter into the Kingdom of Heaven if only he saved."[19] These words, written in the 1920s, allow us to grasp Keynes' view of the imbalances of his day. For Keynes, all problems derived from the fact that humanity is accustomed to frugality and doesn't know how to consume the wealth that capitalism offers. "The principle of saving, pushed to an extreme, would destroy the motive for production. If each person were content with the simplest food, the poorest clothing and the humblest house, it is certain that there would be no other sort of food, clothing, or house."[20]

To get out of underemployment, the remedy is simple: Spend, at all costs, even if this means hiring the unemployed to dig holes in the morning and fill them in the afternoon. Better still, to avoid the crisis multiplier, one has to dissociate the revenue of agents from their employment as much as is possible. In separating jobs and incomes, one thus avoids a situation in which unemployment obliges those who are out of work to reduce their expenditures. One can reduce the multiplier and stabilize the economy.

This is the lesson Keynes drew from the Great Depression. It is not certain that the phenomenon he explained, the theory of the multiplier, really explains the crisis of the 1930s; there were also financial factors. But the idea that capitalism left to itself is profoundly unstable, and the idea that it might be regulated by a skillful economic policy, would be enthusiastically accepted by most governments. After World War II, when they wanted to stabilize the economy, Keynesian remedies would serve as the bible for politicians. The fact that the proposed solution consisted of consuming rather than saving may well be what lies behind the success of these ideas. They would lay the foundation upon which the welfare state would be constructed.

8

THE GOLDEN AGE AND ITS CRISIS

THIRTY GLORIOUS YEARS

In 1946, in a village called Duelle in southwest France, one had to work 24 minutes to buy a kilogram of bread, 45 minutes for a kilogram of sugar, 7 hours for a kilogram of butter, and 8 hours for a kilogram of chicken. Food accounted for three-fourths of total consumption, and half of that was bread and potatoes. Only once a week, on average, did people buy meat from a butcher. Butter was almost unknown. Half the remainder of personal spending was on clothes. Apart from military service, the great majority of the inhabitants made a trip only for a honeymoon or a pilgrimage.

Thirty years later in the same village, the productivity of agricultural work was 12 times as great. Now one worked 85 minutes to buy a kilogram of butter.

The following table shows changes in occupations in Duelle in the three decades.

	1946	1975	
Total population	534	670	
Farmer	208	53	
Non-farm laborers	12	35	
Artisans	27	25	
Employees in service sector	32	102	

At least two babies died per year in 1946; only 0.5 per year in 1975. Adolescents at age 20 were 1.65 meter tall in 1946, 1.71 meter tall in 1975. Only three new houses had been built every 20 years, but 50 were built in 1975. There were five automobiles in 1946, nearly 300 in 1975. And the village went from having two television sets to having 200, from no washing machines to nearly 200, and from five refrigerators to 210.

This famous example opens a now-classic book by Jean Fourastié, *Les Trentes Glorieuses* (1979).[21] Beyond this village, the whole physiognomy of France was transformed in the course of the 30 years separating the end of the war from the mid 1970s. Like Duelle, France as a whole enjoyed, in a very short period of time, all the stages of modern economic growth, including the shift from agriculture to industry and the shift from industry to services.

The great hope of the twentieth century

Duelle is emblematic of the shift from a society in which most of the resources are devoted to feeding people to one in which people go on vacation and watch TV. Through this example, Fourastié reveals what may count as his major discovery, which he shared with the English-speaking world through the work of Colin Clark: Modern society is neither rural nor industrial; in fact, it tends toward a service society. In his first book, *Grand Espoir du XX siècle* (Presses Universitaires de France 1958), Fourastié cites what he thinks is the real sign of progress: "Everything happens as if human labor were in transition from physical effort to mental effort."

The tertiary (service) sector included only 15 percent of jobs in 1820, but today it includes about 75 percent. How can we understand this evolution? The French demographer Alfred Sauvy called it the "spilling" (*déversement*) of employment. It is easier to robotize the work of a factory worker than that of a doctor or a barber. Thus, according to Sauvy, labor inevitably leaves industry and is "spilled" into human activities that are less amenable to mechanization.

The example of the barber who "has been around the world," as Fourastié said proudly in the preface to *Le Grand Espoir*, illustrates how this theory works. The modern barber does more or less the same work as barbers of the Ancien Regime. It is a job in which the benefits of productivity are much weaker than in the textile industry, for example. Over the centuries, though, the salary of a barber has always been almost equal to that of an artisan or a laborer. But the barber does not take part in technical progress, although he benefits from it just as much as does the factory worker who is its artisan. In effect, as long as consumers desire to have their hair cut, a barber can profit from the general rise in wealth and can increase his rates without fearing that a machine will be found to take his place. All he has to worry about is competition from other barbers. But as long as he pegs his rates to the average salary, he can get around this rivalry. This is the foundation of Fourastié's "great hope": In time, only jobs in which a human being is indispensable will remain creditworthy, which is excellent news.

William Baumol used the same reasoning, but with a different twist, when he predicted the decline of live performance.[22] Plays, operas, and concerts of classical music benefit as little from technical progress as do barber shops. Today as yesterday, said Baumol, it takes the same amount of time for Richard II to "tell sad tales of the death of kings." Unlike a barber, though, an actor in a live performance is in direct competition with new entertainment technologies—cinema, cable and satellite TV, DVDs, and so on. Profiting from less costly alternatives, consumers are deserting theaters and concert halls. The lesson is simple: To survive, one must be a user of technical progress or else must work in a sector in which mechanization is impossible. The intermediate situation between the poles (such as the live performance) is the worst. The trend toward the tertiary sector favors the extremes: technology-intensive jobs and jobs that have nothing to do with technology.

THIRTY YEARS LATER

A lot of water has flowed under the bridge since the publication of Jean Fourastié's book. Strictly from an accounting standpoint, there is no doubt that the bulk of employment has gone from industry to the services, just as a century earlier it had gone from agriculture to industry. In 2006—that is, 30 years after the publication of *Les Trente Glorieuses*—the share of industry in overall US employment fell below 10 percent.

However, the tertiary economy is in no way free of the world of stuff. Of course material products cost less to make, and the share of employment devoted to producing them is reduced. But their number continues to increase at the same rate as before, and they have to be moved and repaired. Within the tertiary world, industrial jobs have not disappeared, but workers have become operators or repairers. Employees, many of them women, are cashiers or salespersons. In reality, the world of objects remains just as oppressive.

By all evidence, the great hope for labor freed from the hardship linked to the physical world has certainly not come about, as is attested by the rising number of employees who are suffering from physical pain and who complain about having to move heavy objects.[23] Far from being the paradise dreamed of by Fourastié, the service society, as its name indicates, is the realm of clients who become givers of orders, more so sometimes than the bosses.[24] The hope for a humanist society has ended in major disillusionment. The economy is governed by an ethos of "just in time" imposed by irascible customers who cannot wait to be served.

A changed era

The most troubling thing about that prosperous period in France was the conviction among contemporaries that it would last. Even the French economists who were the most aware of long-range tendencies allowed themselves to believe that growth could continue at the same pace. However, never before had French growth approached the figures it registered during the Thirty Glorious Years. Without even counting the tormented period that followed World War I, French growth had known a pace that today would be considered weak—less than 2 percent a year. How could people have believed in 5 percent a year?

Fourastié was aware that this fortunate era was destined to end. The country could not continue to grow at this pace, he explained, because it was not conceivable that people could consume the mass of stuff thus produced. Here Fourastié repeated the error that he often derided elsewhere: the idea that there might be a physical limit to the human appetite. On the contrary, everything shows that a stomach grows as it is well fed. But another cause of unsustainable growth that Fourastié advanced resonates strongly today. Indefinite growth, especially if it entrains growth in the developing countries, will create new conflicts over the appropriation of the planet's ecology and its rare resources. The shock of the oil price hike appears in his diagnosis, which echoes the Club of Rome's 1972 report *The Limits to Growth*.

However, the economists' current explanation of the ineluctable closure of the three great decades is barely mentioned by Fourastié: the end of France's catching up with the United States. Today we understand that this euphoric sequence marked a period of convergence with the US. In 1945 the per capita income of the French was barely more than one-third that of the Americans. By 1975, the French standard of living had risen to about 75 percent of the American one. This was the real motor. France grew at 5 percent a year, taking 30 years to catch up to the US. It would have spent only 15 years doing so if it had been able to grow at 10 percent a year. This in no way prejudges the long-term dynamic of France's economy, but growth based on imitation of the leader cannot continue indefinitely. Japan had a bitter experience of this in the 1990s. Similarly, China and India are registering rates of growth that are manifestly achieved only thanks to a gap between them and the richest countries, which remains considerable. But their growth will run out of steam, too, as their convergence with the leaders progresses.

Catching up with a country that has already constituted a great stock of technical and organizational expertise is quite different from continuing to grow at a rapid pace once the frontier of knowledge has been reached.[25] During the same postwar period, American growth (which was sustained in comparison with its previous years) attained only 2.5 percent per year on average. To have imagined that French growth could sustainably be twice that rate was obviously naive. But that illusion was shared by almost everyone in France. This explains why it will be many years before France manages to detoxify itself, both economically and politically, from those years of rapid, addictive growth.

9

The End of Solidarities

The Century of the Welfare State

In November of 1940, Winston Churchill commissioned a report about how to fight against both the consequences of the crisis of the 1930s and those entailed by the war then underway. The Beveridge Report, made public in 1942, expounded principles that are still current in Europe today, and which underlie a state's obligations to combat five social evils that Sir William Beveridge enumerated: "Want, Disease, Ignorance, Squalor and Idleness."

Convinced by Keynes that a society cannot become poorer except by not spending enough, Beveridge based his report on the idea that this social expenditure should be guaranteed by the state. Hence its title: *Full Employment in a Free Society*.

The welfare state

The welfare state is not an invention of Beveridge, strictly speaking. The idea preceded the 1930s; without going into detail about its genesis, we may attribute one of its founding principles to Otto von Bismarck. In 1883, Bismarck passed one of the very first social laws designed to help ordinary people, instituting obligatory health insurance for low-wage workers. "Democratic gentlemen," Bismarck famously said, "will play the flute when people realize that the sovereign takes better care of their interests." By the eve of World War I, Great Britain, France, and the United States would all have passed such social laws.

The twentieth century saw the role of the state grow enormously, for which the two world wars were largely responsible. The hike in public spending forced states to increase taxation to unprecedented levels—levels from which they would never descend. And when the world wars were over, social expenditure was slowly but surely substituted for military expenditure.

This rise in the power of public spending didn't really obey a plan, however; it was often forced upon governments. As the French economists Robert Delorme and Christine Andre showed in their book on the French welfare state, *L'État et l'économie*, society gradually claimed rights over education, health, and retirement—which always exceeded any governmental plans.[26] And the welfare state was in crisis from the start. Even if Keynesianism contributed to making this evolution intellectually acceptable, the rise in social spending first corresponded to some perceived need—for health insurance, for old-age pensions—much more than to deliberate Keynesian regulation of activity.

Nothing demonstrates the force of this social demand better than the comparison between the United States and Europe in the health domain. The major part of American health-care spending is by private insurance companies. Yet this spending represents more than 15 percent of the gross domestic product, a figure 50 percent higher than in Europe. Thus, in general, elevated social spending cannot be attributed to the state (and its supposed laxity). It much more certainly reflects the satisfaction of people's needs to be cared for and to be assured of resources for old age—needs that private insurance doesn't fail to meet when the state is not committed to doing so. The demand for health is one of the natural demands of a society that is getting wealthier.[27] Whether insurance is private or public, however, changes nothing about the heart of the problem: This spending must be regulated. The paradox that is often forgotten by those who denigrate the welfare state is that the state is more a policeman than a spendthrift.

This point is particularly clear in the case of health spending. In 1963 the economist Kenneth Arrow summarized the particular problem posed by medical expenses as follows[28]: Health is one of the rare economic goods for which the demand (by the patient) depends entirely on an evaluation made by the person offering the supply (the doctor). The offer indeed dictates the demand, as Jean-Baptiste Say would have said, but for the perverse reason that the person demanding doesn't know what he wants. Anyone who has ever doubted the honesty of his auto repairman knows what Arrow is talking about. But you can always trade in your car; you can't trade in your body. Rarely does anyone dare to argue with a doctor's diagnosis. American econometric studies have quantified the importance of this phenomenon: An increase of 10 percent in the number of doctors in a region contributes to increasing health-care spending in the region by 5.5 percent. The offer is indeed creating its own demand.[29]

To the extent that the nature of health-care spending requires it to be covered by insurance, whether public or private (who would dare to risk dying of appendicitis for want of money?), the perverse mechanism identified by Arrow is reinforced. Not only do people not dare to argue with doctors; the coverage given by the insurance companies doesn't encourage it. In comparison, health care is *more egalitarian* and *less expensive* in Europe than in the United States. Coverage is almost total throughout European countries, whereas 47 million Americans did not have any social coverage before the Obama health-care bill. The reason is simple: The State is really a *brake* on excessive health expenditure rather than responsible for runaway spending.

THE DILEMMA OF GENERATIONS

In the course of the 1980s it gradually became clear that the rapid economic growth of the postwar period would never come back to France or any other country in Western Europe. With the slowing of growth, the crisis in public finances became apparent in many countries. Little by little, all the solidarities that had been shaped in the postwar period were fading, at the very time when they were becoming essential. The American middle class got tired of helping the poor, the Italians in Milan of subsidizing those in Rome, the Flemish in Belgium of financing the Walloons. A 1984 play by Loleh Bellon, *De si tendres liens* [*Such Tender Ties*], may serve as a guide to the nature of the crisis that the decrease in growth has inflicted on the welfare state.

The play concerns two women, a mother and her daughter, during two periods in their lives. In the first period, the mother is a young divorcée and the daughter is a child. All the dialogues in this first period have the same subject: The daughter wants her mother to remain at home and take care of her instead of going out with men at night. The second period is 25 years later (though the play is constructed in such a way that we can't immediately tell when the dialogues are taking place). The daughter's preoccupations are her husband, her children, and her work. The mother has gotten old and has remained alone. The dialogues relating to this period also have a single subject: The mother demands that her daughter remain with her and not abandon her to solitude.

The genius of this play is the continual alternation between the two periods. Twenty-five years apart, it is the same dialogue that is spoken, but with the roles reversed. Each of these two women, at two distinct moments, demands the same thing: to be loved by the other. If they were the same age, the problem would be simple; their reciprocal love would be strengthened in the here and now. The difficulty of loving across the generations comes from the fact that (as an economist would put it) there is never a coincidence between wants.

Bellon's play makes this frustration all the more troubling because she also shows how simple it would be for this mother to give more time to her daughter, and the daughter more time to her mother. It seems that it would take very little for this reciprocal love to be free of the shackles imposed by the gap in ages. It would suffice for these women to have access to what happens in families in which people of all ages love one another. When parents love their children and their own parents, the chain of the generations is never broken.

But the women in *De si tendres liens* are caught in a relationship that is a duel. The mother doesn't love her daughter enough (and is trying to get remarried) because she knows (fears) that later her daughter will turn away from her to lead her own adult life. It would take a bridge—a durable institution, the "family"—for children to transmit the love of their parents to their own children and to give it back to their parents. In the absence of this intergenerational chain, each person certainly may love the other, of course, but the frustration dramatized by Bellon prevents this love from being free of the constraints of the here and now.

In the cold language of economics, one would say that the mother and the daughter are constrained to an "inefficient" affective exchange. Each is unhappy, but each could love the other more. A model we owe to Paul Samuelson and to Maurice Allais, which plays an essential role in modern economic analysis, perfectly illustrates the mechanisms in this drama.[30]

To understand the logic at work here, let us return to the story of Robinson Crusoe. Alone on his island, he knows that he will be less able to fish when he is old. To prepare for his retirement, he could make a large number of fishing rods, but he will never know the right number. Worn out with fatigue, he will die early, because he cannot fish as he used to when he was young. Suppose, though, that a "new Crusoe" arrives on the island every 25 years on average. The new Crusoe knows nothing about the old one; each leads a solitary life. The young Crusoe sees the old one failing, incapable of feeding himself. He could help him, out of human generosity. But as with the women in Bellon's play, his generosity has limits. He has to think of himself, too, and prepare for his own old age.

Let us suppose that the island sets a rule: The young Crusoes must give the old ones a share (say 10 percent) of their income. The contribution demanded by the state allows them to accomplish a new intergenerational exchange. All the Crusoes, young and old, benefit from this exchange. As in a family in which there is inter-generational love, each gives to the preceding generations what he will receive from the succeeding generations.

This is exactly how distributive pension systems work. Those no longer working receive the contributions of those who are still working. If the young ones to come are richer, thanks to rapid growth, it will be more advantageous for them to trade 10 percent of their current income for the promise of receiving in exchange 10 percent from the generations to come. This property of the "pay as you go" distributive pension system explains why it was supported by a refer-endum during the Thirty Glorious Years. The more rapid the growth, the more people are ready to cede the fruits of their labor to the state.

The (new) crisis of public finance

A strange paradox is taking shape. Strong growth makes us believe in the possibility of an enduring link between the generations. The welfare state creates a chain of financial solidarity that tends to take the place of the family. We can be less concerned about our parents when they are financially independent. Alas, the chain of solidar-ity created by the welfare state weakens when growth slows. Then everything is lost; family solidarity has disintegrated and the welfare state becomes a financial burden.

This reasoning enables us to understand—beyond the example of insurance in old age—the crisis in public finance that began to hit industrial countries in the 1970s when growth slowed. Contrary to the reasoning popularized by the heirs of Keynes, it appears today that strong growth enabled public expenditures to rise, not that the expenditures engendered growth. Deprived of rapid growth, the welfare state had to learn to count what it spent. Governments had to arbitrate between various demands: health or education, the army or pensioners. Taxes and social security contributions are harder to raise when growth is slowing. Governments painfully awoke to the reality of a new budgetary constraint, since the past euphoria had led them to believe, too, in the possibility of a perpetual solidarity between generations.

The Impossible Search for Happiness

The despair that the end of the Thirty Glorious Years caused in French society illuminates a basic trait of modern society: its addiction to growth. This goes farther than encouraging public spending; it touches the personal happiness of individuals. The French were incomparably richer in 1975 than in 1945, but they were not happier. Why do they have so many regrets? The answer is simple. The happiness of modern-day people is not proportionate to the standard of wealth attained, but depends on its growth, whatever its point of departure may be.

In 1974 the economist Richard Easterlin published a study that made a big splash and drew the attention of economists to this point.[31] By tracking the answers to a survey question "Are you happy?" over 30 years, Easterlin showed that no change was observed despite formidable enrichment during the period covered. How can we understand this paradox?

Let us deal first with the basic question. What is happiness? In 1960, 65 percent of Americans questioned mentioned finances, 48 percent health, and 47 percent family. Thirty years later, the figures had scarcely changed. Earning a good living was mentioned by 75 percent of those surveyed. Fifty percent mentioned a successful family. Health had lost a bit of ground; only one-third mentioned it. War and peace, freedom, and equality were mentioned by less than 10 percent of the respondents. And the figures are astonishingly stable from one country and one kind of regime to another. In Cuba in 1960, for example, the corresponding figures were 73 percent money, 53 percent family, and 47 percent health; in Yugoslavia at the same time, they were 83 percent money, 60 percent family, and 40 percent health.

If wealth is so important an element in happiness, why does a society that is getting richer seem to fail to make its members happier?

The simplest explanation is that consumption is like a drug. I can no longer do without certain goods, even though I was ignorant of their existence 10 years earlier. The cell phone and access to the Internet become indispensable once people discover them. Consumption creates dependence. The pleasure things give is ephemeral, but the despair when one is deprived of them is terrible. These intuitions are confirmed by a large number of recent studies. The work of Daniel Kahneman and Amos Tversky and that of Andrew Clark show that an increase in income makes people happy, but that the satisfaction drawn from a higher income evaporates quickly. According to these studies, it has decreased by 60 percent after only two years. Analyses of the behavior of voters are even more startling. Voters seem to remember only the economic situation of the last six months.

The first explanation doesn't exhaust the question, though. In a given society, the wealthy are indeed happier. If addiction were the sole cause, the wealthy would be as bored as the poor. But 90 percent of the wealthiest respond that they are "very" or "somewhat" happy, while only 65 percent of the poorest answer that they are. This result is confirmed by many surveys. The majority of people who are financially comfortable are always very happy. If all this were just an addiction to wealth, this would not be the case.

The explanation of this result is not surprising and relates to a simple and eternal phenomenon: envy. People enjoy doing better than others. As Marx observed, "A house may be large or small; as long as the neighboring houses are likewise small, it satisfies all social requirement for a residence. But let there arise next to the little house a palace, and the little house shrinks to a hut. The little house now makes it clear that its inmate has no social position at all to maintain."[32] Each person tries to do better than his or her colleagues or friends—those who form one's "reference group." Experimental studies using games show that people are ready to use a share of their profits to reduce the profits of other participants in the same game. Clark shows that there is even sometimes a negative correlation between work satisfaction and the salary of a spouse.[33]

More recently, Easterlin has offered another explanation that complements the preceding one. For him, everything starts at school. The young begin their adult lives with aspirations that are initially closer to those of their fellow young people, whatever their social origin. When one asks them what goods they would like to own, all of them reply that they want—in this order—a car, a house, a garden, a high-definition TV, and so on. The correlation between the aspirations of the young and the income level of the parents is almost nil. But in adulthood, each person (rich or poor) ends up indexing his aspiration to the reality with which he is confronted. With time, ambitions (high or low) get stuck around the position that the person occupies in the social scale. But because the rich have realized their childhood dreams, and because the poor have been frustrated in theirs, the rich are happier.

Another point (perhaps a cynical one) should be made here. Although according to Easterlin's interpretation the children of the rich are happier in proportion to the time shared with children of the poor, it is better to leave them together as long as possible. Raising rich children in "rich ghettos" deprives them of the pleasure of exceeding their aspirations. Thus their world becomes as sad as that of the poor.

Overall, whether out of envy or dream-wishes, each of us indexes his or her aspirations to those of a reference group that he or she wants to imitate. It may be that this group is large at the start of one's life (including cousins and children in the same school class), but with time the reference group is most often reduced to a few close friends who share one's social destiny. When the careers of two friends diverge, it becomes very difficult for them to share activities. What vacations, and what restaurants, can two people share when one is rich and the other poor? The divergence of material destinies segments the world of the affective life.

However one evaluates these results, a simple and brutal conclusion remains: Economic growth gives each person a hope, even though it may be ephemeral, of getting out of his situation, catching up with others, or exceeding his or her expectations. It is the *improvement* of personal situations that makes a society happy. Modern societies are more avid for *growth* than for wealth. Thus it is better to live in a poor country that is getting rich quickly than in a rich country that is stagnating. The French enjoyed the Thirty Glorious Years because everything was new. But the page always stays blank on the happiness yet to be conquered. As rapid as the economic growth may be at any moment in time, frustration inevitably catches up with a society when that growth slows.

Epithemeus

The inexhaustible need to compare oneself with others doesn't come as a surprise to economists who have read Adam Smith's *Theory of Moral Sentiments*, the major conclusion of which, as we have seen, is that human desire is always "to be observed, to be attended to, to be taken notice of with sympathy and approbation. . . . It is the vanity, not the ease, or the pleasure, which interests us." It would not surprise a specialist in Greek mythology, either. This insatiable appetite is the punishment that the gods inflicted on men to neutralize the Promethean power stolen from them. As Jean-Pierre Vernant notes in *The Universe, Gods, and Mortals*,[34] "Before [Prometheus] intervened, [men] were living like ants in caves . . . and then, thanks to him, they became civilized beings, distinct from the beasts and distinct from the gods. . . . Zeus withheld fire, Prometheus stole it from him." To take revenge, Zeus comes up with a fatal trap for man: Pandora.

> Pandora possesses the beauty of the immortal goddesses; her appearance is divine. . . . Radiant like Aphrodite, and also, like a child of Night, made up of lies and coquetry. . . . Prometheus sees he is beaten again.

He understands instantly what's being dangled before the nose of the poor human race that he has been trying to help. As his name "Pro-metheus" indicates, he is foresighted, the one who understands a situation beforehand, who anticipates, whereas his brother "Epi-metheus" is the one who understands only afterward— *epi*, too late—who is always taken in and let down, who never sees it coming.

The tragedy of the modern world now opens.

In this case Prometheus sees what is going to happen and he warns his brother: "Listen, Epithemeus, if ever the gods send you a gift, absolutely do not accept it, send it right back where it came from." Epithemeus swears of course that he won't be fooled. But then the assembled gods send him the loveliest person in the world. Before him stands Pandora, the god's gift to mankind. She knocks at his door, and Epithemeus—in wonderment, bedazzled—opens it to her and brings her into his home. The next day he is married and Pandora is established as a wife among the humans. And thus begin all their miseries. She is always dissatisfied, demanding, self-indulgent. She is never content with what there is; she wants to be sated, surfeited.

The Greeks, as we see, excuse themselves for their own turpitude at the expense of their wives. "Woman is two different things at once," Vernant writes in his commentary on this myth. "She is the belly devouring everything her husband has laboriously gathered at the cost of his effort, his toil, his fatigue, but that belly is also the only one that can produce the thing that extends man's life, a child."

What remains extraordinary, once the terrible misogyny of this myth is overcome, is the astonishing image of the human adventure that it offers. Though modern myth has freed Prometheus from his chains, it is in the guise of Epithemeus that modern man leads his ordinary life, inhabited by an ever-present tension between fecundity and voracity, understanding too late the fate to which this conflict leads. Such is the weakness of a civilization that believes it is guided by the calculation of its interest: Only afterward is it aware what has happened to it. The West never understood, in real time, its economic growth, or the crisis of the 1930s, or the postwar boom. Very often, as was the case with Malthus' Law, the West grasps the laws only after they have become a dead letter. The West acts first; only later does it try to understand the chain reaction it has unleashed.

10

WAR AND PEACE

KONDRATIEFF CYCLES

People's happiness depends on the gap between their aspirations and the reality they discover in real life. Transposed to the geopolitical order, this raises the following question: Are wars engendered by misery or by boredom, by crises, or by prosperity? The two world wars of the twentieth century suggest different answers.

World War I arrived during a time of prosperity; World War II was engendered by the crisis of 1929. Each war illuminates one aspect of the question of how wars start. To grasp the nature of the problem, let us follow the chronology, both insightful and whimsical, established 60 years ago by the Russian economist Nicolas Kondratieff.[35] Stalin deported Kondratieff at the end of the 1920s because his theory supposedly contradicted the Marxist theory of the tendency of capitalism to decline. His own chronology was thus interrupted after World War I. But it is difficult to resist the fascination of number series and of extrapolating from them.

Kondratieff observed that economic activity seems to have a periodicity of 50 years, with 25 years of growth followed (on average) by 25 years of crisis, then another 25 years of growth, and so on. He thus revealed three great cycles that have occurred since the Industrial Revolution at the end of the eighteenth century. By forcing the figures a bit, we get the following dating for cycles:

1789–1823 growth; 1824–1848 crisis and end of first cycle

1849–1873 growth; 1874–1898 crisis and end of second cycle

1899–1923 growth; 1924–1948 crisis and end of third cycle.

Let us continue Kondratieff's scheme:

1949–1973 growth; 1974–1998 crisis and end of fourth cycle

1999–2023 growth; 2024–2048 crisis and end of fifth cycle.

According to this chronology, we have entered the fifth cycle, and 1998–2023 should be a period of growth. And that makes the sub-prime crisis only an aberration.

Few present-day economists subscribe to the scheme proposed by Kondratieff. It may sometimes work for one country, but not for another, and the need for 25-year fluctuations is difficult to understand by any scientific hypothesis. However, the idea of long cycles, whatever intellectual acrobatics they may lead to, remains fascinating. Despite Kondratieff's approximations—the 1929 crisis being heralded in 1923, and the exit from the current crisis predicted for 1998—it testifies to a respiration pattern that is indisputable. No society can remain forever on the tightrope of regular growth. The highs and lows of economic activity make precious correlations appear for whoever tries to understand the articulation between economic cycles and political and military cycles.

———

Kondratieff himself noted certain coincidences. He observed that wars are more numerous during periods of expansion. Inversely, periods of recession are more favorable to peace. Revolutions occur during periods of turnaround, when the crisis yields to growth. Writing after World War II, Gaston Imbert, a faithful reader of Kondratieff, established a correlation between economic cycles and the political and social processes that confirm these observations.[36] Let us take up his story from the revolutionary wars to World War I.

At the summit of the first cycle at the start of the nineteenth century, Europe lived through the hectic Napoleonic campaigns. The defeat at Waterloo marked the start of the turnaround. The Congress of Vienna, orchestrated by Metternich, organized the peace in Europe but led to a politically reactionary mood that was incarnated in France by the reign of Charles X. The European economy entered a long phase of deflation and price lowering. This deflation made the scales of history incline toward creditors (*rentiers*), while those in debt—including nation-states—suffered. The only option of indebted governments seemed to be to pay back debts they had contracted during the Napoleonic Wars. Until the middle of the nineteenth century, budgetary and political conservatism reigned, one reinforcing the other. This coincided with peace among nations.

In 1848, the movement was the reverse, and the breathing period changed cadence. Louis-Philippe of France was deposed, and Metternich fled Austria. Gold was discovered in California and in Australia. Prices were on an upward slope. Inflation favored investors and those who went into debt. In parallel, the tone of politics changed. The years 1848–1873 saw the appearance of Marxism and the rediscovery of the myths of the French Revolution. Society was agitated, getting rid of the guardians of the orthodoxy that it had adopted in the wake of the Congress of Vienna. In politics, a new generation came along that had been only 10 years old in 1810 and so had no aversion to armed conflicts. Wars followed one another in quick succession: the Crimean war, the Italian war, the American Civil War, wars between Prussia and Denmark, between Austria and France, and between Austria and Italy, and finally the war between Prussia and France in 1870.

And then history let itself be carried along by its pendulum movement. The year 1873 saw the Kondratieff cycle enter its downward swing; again the crisis lasted 25 years, and the period 1873–1897 is sometimes called by historians "the great depression."[37] Once more, the value system was inverted. A wind of peace blew over European nations, and the rare wars that flared up were confined to the periphery. The crisis revived the conservative morality of small savers. In the words of Gaston Imbert, "The low period, a time of political and social tranquility, appears to us strangely peaceful. The economic regression, reducing profits, in fact did purify manners: There was less divorce, children were more numerous and fewer of them were abandoned, abortions diminished. With the decrease in prices, the number of crimes fell, and the social organism became calmer."

Everything changed again with the start of a new Kondratieff cycle. In 1898, in France, the crusading writer Emile Zola and President Clemenceau reopened the Dreyfus Affair, which challenged the legal and military systems. Gold was discovered in Alaska and in South Africa. The steam engine and the railway were succeeded by the automobile and electricity. The happy carousel of history resumed its amnesiac course. People sang about growth and went back to war: the Sino-Japanese war (1895, a little in advance), the Spanish-American War (1898), the Boer War (1899), the Greco-Turkish war

(1897), the Russo-Japanese War (1903–04), the Italo-Turkish War (1911), the Balkan War (1912), then World War I (which was the worthy heir of the Napoleonic Wars, and which occurred at the height of the growth period).

This frenetic cavalcade suggests a lesson. Economic cycles and military cycles are closely linked. Conflicts are unleashed, including World War I, in the high periods of Kondratieff cycles. Inversely, in crisis periods the state draws in upon itself. What is the source of this correlation between war and prosperity, and why does World War II invalidate it?

ECONOMICS AND POLITICS

A Keynesian analysis of the correlation between war and growth would go as follows: Military expenditures create new outlets for business. Wars propel economic growth; peace triggers recession, depriving the economy of weapons expenditures and slowing growth. Alvin Hansen, the first American Keynesian, noted this phenomenon and drew from it the practical recommendation that to eliminate economic cycles entirely it sufficed to avoid the second phase (in which states seek to pay back their war debts and reduce their spending).

This interpretation is not enough, however, for wars stimulate growth, not the reverse. As Gaston Imbert shows, wars generally start *at the end* of the growth cycle, rather than at the beginning.[38] According to a British author who has also observed this, "Sparks fly in the second stage of expansion."[39] It is growth that pushes toward war.

Several theories aid in understanding this linkage. The theory of imperialism is one. Lenin's idea, taken up by Hannah Arendt, is that the bourgeoisie, when it gradually takes control of the affairs of state, pushes for war in order to protect its supplies of raw materials and to find colonial markets. However, as Schumpeter emphasizes, it is not on the orders of the bourgeoisie that states conduct their wars, even if that class finds an interest in increasing its commercial preserves.[40] Rather, governments conduct wars on their own account, for purposes of power. The motives for war linked to the economy are no less numerous in periods of recession than in periods of expansion. In effect, it is during recession periods that it becomes more urgent to protect markets. Economic wars, like protectionist measures, are often produced in phases of recession.

Another theory accounts better for the way growth feeds the appetite for war among states. It follows the reasoning offered by Paul Kennedy in *The Rise and Fall of the Great Powers*.[41] For Kennedy, economic wealth enables military power to be expressed. According to his theory of imperial overstretch, the great powers are pushed to run through all their wealth in order to defend their status. This corresponds to the fiscal history of European states, which shows (as we have seen) how they let themselves be asphyxiated by the cost of war and how they are always overcome by the spiraling of new military technologies. Whereas Lenin, looking at the nineteenth century, saw the hand of the bourgeoisie pushing states to protect their markets, Kennedy finds that it is the state that desires power, and that the state takes advantage of its bourgeoisie to accomplish its own designs.

On this line of reasoning, the role of growth becomes clear. It releases the budgetary constraints on states and enables them to achieve their own ambitions. The effects of international trade on war may be interpreted according to the same analysis. To the extent that trade may enable one nation in a state of latent war with another one to diversify its supply sources, it may contribute to making new wars possible. Such is the main conclusion of a study by Philippe Martin, Thierry Mayer, and Mathias Thoenig that runs counter to the optimistic ideas that Montesquieu formulated nearly 300 years ago.[42]

Private happiness and public happiness

Schumpeter criticized Lenin's position on the responsibility of capitalism for the European wars. For Schumpeter, colonial goals and (generally speaking) bellicose inclinations are by no means inevitable consequences of the capitalist system. Instead, they result from certain survivals of the pre-capitalist mentality that are strongly rooted in the ruling classes of the main European powers. It is inconceivable, Schumpeter says, that capitalism as such should lead to conquest and war, for everything about it is "rationality and calculation."

The idea that wars are born from a conflict between different types of mentality is very illuminating. But what Schumpeter seems to ignore is that these mentalities often coexist in a contradictory way within the same people. *Homo economicus*, cold and rational, stripped of any passion, is a fiction to which Adam Smith himself never subscribed. At the end of his book *The Passions and the Interests*, Albert Hirschman ironically refers his opponent Schumpeter to a remark made by Jean-François-Paul de Gondi, Cardinal of Retz: "A truly subtle politician does not wholly reject the conjectures which one can derive from man's passions, for passions enter sometimes rather openly into . . . the motives that propel the important affairs of state."[43]

A theory offered by Hirschman in another book can help us grasp how individuals modify their value systems to correspond to economic circumstances.[44] Hirschman's theory echoes Easterlin's theory concerning happiness. According to Hirschman, individuals consume two types of goods: the usual private goods (including lodging, clothing, food, and leisure) and public goods (those one shares with others). In this latter category are all the great collective projects: anti-poverty programs, space exploration, wars, and so on. In Hirschman's terms, as in Easterlin's, it is not the *level* of wealth that decides whether one prefers private goods to collective goods; rather, it is the gap between individuals' expectations and their realization. Reducing available income by one-third may make people very unhappy; an unexpected hike of one-third can make them marvelously satisfied. (These figures are from Alfred Sauvy.) But when wealth falls below their expectations, people are frustrated, feel themselves to be poor, and become individualists. Inversely, as soon as they are surprised by wealth that exceeds their aspirations, people are much more ready to share the surplus that falls into their laps. Public goods become attractive again.

Thus, people want collective happiness in periods of growth, when the goods of private consumption are abundant and when private happiness tends (provisionally) to be secure. Inversely, when economic expansion is weak and goods to consume are more rare, the collective welfare becomes a costly luxury, and people vaunt the values of the individual and the sober pleasures of family life. Thus, there is a moral type for the "fat years" and a moral type for the "lean years": the 1960s on the one side, the 1980s on the other. The former praise the collective, the latter angelicize the individual.

If the periods of strong growth engender a "social surplus" suitable for collective actions, the use that will be made of that surplus still remains contingent on the political history of each country. The Germany of the Kaiser used its profits to construct a navy able to rival England's. The US of Presidents Kennedy and Johnson wanted both to outstrip the USSR (in Vietnam and in the race to the moon) and to pursue a "New Frontier" of social and civil rights.

Periods of turnaround produce the exactly opposite effects. A society that undergoes weaker-than-forecast growth, or even a major recession, will not be poor, but its surplus will disappear, and the ethos will become one of every man for himself. The paradox is that just when social solidarity is most necessary, in bad times, it becomes most difficult to maintain. The slowing of growth after the Thirty Glorious Years illustrates this perfectly. The solidarities between religions, and between generations, seemed harder to support, although the societies concerned were much wealthier than they were 30 years previously.

Thus the intrinsic fragility of industrial societies is played out in a difficult articulation between high-growth and low-growth periods. Growth gives states the means to achieve their old geopolitical ambitions. In contrast, a crisis weakens society. When the economy turns sour, finding support, economically and morally, from the wealth accumulated during periods of growth appears to be impossible. Society becomes divided, and every scenario becomes possible. The sociologist Ernest Gellner summarized this situation perfectly: "[A society of] sustained and perpetual growth [buys off] social aggression with material enhancement; its greatest weakness is its inability to survive any temporary reduction of the social bribery fund, and to weather the loss of legitimacy which

---

befalls it if the cornucopia becomes temporarily jammed and the flow falters."[45]

World War II testifies to this sequence, but not in a typical way. When Hitler came to power, it was quite evident that neither England nor France, each weakened by the economic crisis, wanted war (and, as they showed at Munich, they were willing to forestall it at almost any price). The economic crisis had removed their desire for war. Peace and recession were supposed to go together, but Hitler understood the tragic dilemma first and offered Germany an external solution to its domestic problems.

Evidently World War II exceeds all the mechanical interpretations that could be given of it. The moral collapse of Germany could never be deduced from solely objective causes, such as the fallout from the Treaty of Versailles or the 1929 crisis. It escapes "rationality and calculation." As the German philosopher Ernst Cassirer said in April 1945, "In all critical moments of social life, the forces of reason, which stand against the reawakening of old mythic ideas, are no longer sure of themselves. [Myth] is biding its time, waiting for its opportunity. Its hour comes as soon as the other cohesive forces in societal life, for one reason or another, lose their power and are no longer able to fight against demonic forces."[46] This statement, intended as an epitaph for a history that has ended, assumed a tragic currency just before the dawn of the twenty-first century.

III

THE TIME OF GLOBALIZATION

11

The Return of India and China

The Great Divergence

Twentieth-century history resumed its march. Between the death of Mao and the fall of the Berlin Wall, a new phenomenon called *globalization* reset the counter of human history to zero. What instituted it can be summarily expressed as the return of India and China to the game of world capitalism. Despite ideas that circulated a few years earlier, the cultural specificities of those countries did *not* pose insurmountable resistance to the reign of the market. To grasp the exceptional scope of this turning point, let us return to the reasons why these two great civilizations had been eclipsed by Europe in the course of the three previous centuries, before we move on to how they returned to the table of world capitalism.

The East and the West

Hegel and then Marx popularized the idea that Asia lived under the iron rule of "oriental despots." It was said that their omnipotence blocked Asia's evolution toward the modernism of the West, with its ideas of individual initiative and representative political institutions. These ideas were taken up in part by Max Weber, who characterized the evolution of the West as a "rationalization" of the economic world and of social life, separating public space from private space and resulting in a legal and rational bureaucracy.[1] Weber certainly knew about the commercial activity of the Chinese and the Indians, but he argued that only the West had learned to master commercial relations in a rational way, as witnessed by the discovery of double-entry bookkeeping.

Still, the density of the Asiatic population shows that Asia had no reason to be envious of Europe. According to Malthus' reasoning, the more populated a society, the more it demonstrates that it has learned to resolve the agricultural problems that usually curtail demographic expansion. From an industrial viewpoint, Indian cotton factories and Chinese silk and porcelain mills proved that Asia was a past master of manufacturing production, and well before England. Traders had been traveling around the Indian Ocean for a long time when the East India Company began to rival them. As the economic historian Kenneth Pomeranz emphasizes in his book *The Great Divergence*, this Asian zone was a paradise of *laissez-faire*, with ports such as Calcutta in India and Melaka in Malaysia much more liberal than their European counterparts.[2] Neither the Mogul Empire in India nor the Qing (Manchu) Dynasty in China was the idle state that Westerners imagined. They were complex multi-ethnic empires, much more sophisticated than that of the Austrian Hapsburgs.

These two civilizations had long possessed a depth and a wealth unequalled in Europe. In 1000 CE, India and China represented more than half of the world's wealth and more than half of its population, Europe only 10 percent of either. China was ahead of the West in practically everything. It already mastered the iron plough and the crossbow. It knew lacquer, kites (including kites for lifting humans), the compass, paper, steel, the use of petroleum and natural gas as fuels, horse harnesses, wheelbarrows, and canals. Their alchemic research allowed the Chinese to invent gunpowder, and their fascination with magnetism led them to discover the compass, which enabled them to make daring voyages, such as Admiral Zhang He's trip to Africa in the early fifteenth century.

In the seven volumes of his masterwork, *Science and Civilization in China*,[3] Joseph Needham posed the critical question: Why did modern science, that of Galileo and Newton, develop in the West and not in China? What hidden obstacle hindered its advance? The Chinese developed hydraulic clocks but did not proceed to mechanical clocks—and not for lack of interest, for they were fascinated with them when the Europeans presented them as gifts. Their gunpowder was used not for military purposes but for fireworks. Gunpowder became effective in Europe only after many inventions. It would take many adaptations before the cannonball became more murderous for the person who received it than for the person who shot it.

Why didn't the Chinese manage to unleash the same growth process as the Europeans, when their starting conditions were so much better? Several explanations have been offered.

The ambiguous roles of markets and the state

To explain the economic success of England after the seventeenth century, Douglas North and others have emphasized the quality of its institutions: the respect for private property, the solvency of the state, effective markets, and so on. However, one must conclude from the evicence cited by Pomeranz that these institutions were also present in eighteenth-century China. Neither the state nor market development can explain Chinese backwardness.

Let us begin with the oft-defended idea that in Asia and the Islamic world the state was too powerful for the rich merchants to feel truly secure.[4] In fact, from the available data it is not certain that the expropriation of merchants was more common in Asia than in Europe, where the long royal tradition of repudiating public debts is well documented. In fact, the Chinese state borrowed very little. Having less need of money, it was less constrained to grant monopolies on trade in salt, tobacco, and alcohol, as was the case in Europe.

Nor was Asiatic backwardness with respect to ownership of land and work flagrant. A large share of land was as marketable in China, as in Europe. Some lands, especially in the north, belonged in theory to the state and were rented out on a hereditary basis, but these lands represented only 3 percent of the total. They were, *de facto*, considered to be the property of those who held the deeds to them.[5]

The same parallel is apparent in the labor market. Servile labor that attached serfs to owners rapidly lost ground in China at about the same time as in Western Europe. The hereditary system that obliged a son to have the same occupation as his father began to

---

disintegrate in the fifteenth century, and the Qing formally abolished it in 1695. During the transition between the Ming and Qing dynasties, around 1620, most of the workers who were still serfs were liberated thanks to war and to the chaos and the manpower shortage that followed it. Chinese peasants, in fact, encountered far fewer obstacles than their European counterparts in shifting from working the land to artisanship. With respect to textiles, the Chinese corporations were weak. The Qing strongly encouraged women in the countryside to engage in industrial production. In France, not until the Revolution was the power of corporations dissolved.[6]

Even in the realm of "consumer society" Europe doesn't seem to have been ahead of China. Between 1400 and 1800 there was similar evolution in the number of ostentatious objects that magnified a person's status. During the Ming Dynasty (1368–1644), the interiors of wealthier Chinese houses were covered with paintings and precious furniture. Since social status could be attained through the purchase of refined consumer goods rather than through bloodlines, books on "good taste" multiplied in China, as in Europe. A "treatise of superfluous things" published during this period helped the aristocracy to adopt the new fashion system, teaching it how to distinguish itself from the vulgarity of the *nouveaux riches*.

History and geography

In the fourteenth century China enjoyed an industrial revolution very similar to the one England initiated four centuries later. Thanks to an agricultural revolution linked to the planting of Vietnamese rice species, there was rapid urbanization. Textile and steel manufacturing developed.[7] China was at the door of the Industrial Revolution. The Chinese had understood the principle of atmospheric pressure for a long time, so from a strictly technical point of view they were perfectly able to develop the steam engine. Why didn't they do so?

According to Pomeranz, a geographical accident was the main reason. The north and the northwest of China possessed (and still possess) vast reserves of coal. The Chinese had mastered the transformation of coal into coke (purified coal). China produced more coal for metallurgical purposes in the year 1000 than did Europe (apart from Russia) in 1700. But the Mongol invasion that occurred at the start of the fourteenth century upset the empire. When China recovered some stability after 1420, the demographic and economic center of the country had shifted to the south. Extraction of coal resumed in the north, but it never became again a dynamic sector on the forefront of innovations. The potential users of coal in the south and the producers in the north did not intersect.

David Landes offers another explanation, a cultural one.[8] He explains that China gradually got bogged down in philosophical and political immobility under the Ming Dynasty. Given the disorder that followed the Mongol invasion, the search for domestic stability became a priority, and exploration of the world was shoved into the background. Despite the zebras and giraffes brought back from Africa by Admiral Zhang He, the emperor decided that voyages such as his were costly and useless.

This policy would discourage trade and industry and would favor corruption and nepotism. Étienne Balazs, quoted by Landes, summarizes this quest for immobility as an obsessive need to control the empire.[9] As in a totalitarian state, as we would say today, the state dictated everything, from education to trade. "The atmosphere of routine, traditionalism and immobility made any innovation suspect."

China didn't benefit from the stimulus represented in Europe by the rivalry between European powers. Preoccupied by internal stability, China interrupted the dynamic that it had commenced much earlier. A few decades before Christopher Columbus embarked for America, China chose stability and closed in on itself. Europe took the other path.

THE RETURN OF CHINA

In *A History of Civilizations* Fernand Braudel recounts the stupefaction of a British traveler in China in the eighteenth century "at the sight of a ship being transferred from one level of water to another without going through a lock, but simply being lifted by human strength." This anecdote, which summarizes many others, leads Braudel to comment: "No task was too hard for human beings. And in China they came so cheap."[10] This is substantially what frightens people today about China's re-appearance on the international scene: 1.3 billion people ready to work for almost nothing, forming a huge industrial reserve army such as Marx could never have imagined.

The speed with which China has passed from the status of an economy cut off from the rest of the world to one of the most commercially open economies in the world is stupefying. It is now the world's number-two economy, behind the United States and ahead of Japan. Today economic analysts spend much of their intellectual energy making an inventory of the sectors in which China is an exporter, and mourning for its competitors. These sectors include textiles, toys, televisions, and some unexpected products. Erik Izraelewicz's book *Quand la Chine change le monde* (*When China Changes the*

World) offers a baroque list of items with which Chinese products compete, including truffles from Perigord and granite from Brittany.[11]

Commercial surpluses enable China to accumulate huge exchange revenue that places it far ahead of other industrial countries, on a par with the great petroleum-exporting countries. China holds, in liquid reserves, the equivalent of France's GDP. These reserves give it the means of a new power. China subsidizes Africa and pays tribute to the great international organizations—in which it intends to take its rightful place soon.

It is easy to be impressed by the speed with which China may become the richest country in the world. Extrapolation from the current rates suggest that this will happen sometime between 2030 and 2050. According to Goldman Sachs it may happen as early as 2030. The Centre d'Etudes Prospectives et d'Informations Internationales is more cautious. Taking care to reduce expected growth in proportion to wealth, the CEPII foresees that China will not reach the top until 2050.

This expected upset is obviously connected to the size of China's population. In per capita income, China remains a poor country. In the international classifications, it is at the level of Egypt, with a standard of living equivalent to that of an American in 1913. When (let us say in 2050) it becomes the richest country in the world, its per capita income will be equal to that of an American in the 2000s. Measured in years, the disparity in per capita income between China and the United States will go from 150 years in 1900 to 50 years in 2050.

The new workshop of the world

Upon the death of Mao, the Chinese authorities decided that the economy should be transformed. After the elimination of the Gang of Four, Deng Xiaoping set China on a path toward a market economy. He did so by proceeding in several stages, which were nicely conceived from a political standpoint and somewhat astonishing from an economic standpoint. The first stage consisted of liberalizing the prices of agricultural products, which caused a rapid rise in peasant revenue, which had long been stifled by artificially low prices. One might have thought, at this stage of the transition, that the regime would finally be favorable to peasants, and sensitive to the argument of the Physiocrats that the only road to long-lasting enrichment is via prosperous agriculture. Nothing of the sort. Very quickly, economic policy took an almost opposite path, encouraging massive development of the industrial sector to the detriment of the rural populations.

Privatization of land seemed the next logical stage in the process of liberalization, but it did not take place. Not until 2008 did a debate over private ownership of land occur. Now the economy and politics followed opposite paths. The privatization of land would have permitted increasing agrarian productivity. But the government's concern was to keep peasants from selling their land, which would have resulted in a mass exodus to the cities.[12] This restriction of access to rural ownership was exactly identical to what Japan had done in the nineteenth century—and it was done for the same reason. As a result, Chinese agricultural productivity would remain weak. After the first phase, when price liberalization enabled peasants to get rich quickly, their income made little progress.

The resemblance between the Chinese strategy and the previous Japanese one goes beyond the rural issue. The Chinese strategy, essentially a copy of Japan's, can be summarized as having three prongs. The first consists of keeping a systematically undervalued currency in order to stimulate exports. The promotion of exports is a policy constant in most Asian countries. It was tried and tested in Japan first, then in Taiwan, South Korea, Hong Kong, and Singapore. Adam Smith explained that the major ingredient of sustainable growth pertains to the development of markets, the absence of which would supposedly be the main handicap of poor countries. The global market now makes it possible to avoid this obstacle, just as British development did in the nineteenth century.

The second prong of the Chinese policy, also imported from Japan, relates to an intensive education system. The Maoist strategy for schools bore fruit. Launched in the middle of the 1950s, it allowed China to reduce the illiteracy rate to one-third of the population at the start of the 1980s. This policy was then reinforced by a law, passed in 1986, that required at least 9 years of education after the age of 6. By 2023, the number of Chinese citizens speaking English may exceed the number of people for whom English is the native language.

The third prong is a very high savings level, close to 50 percent. Such a rate finances investment at a frenetic rate and results in considerable foreign reserves. This plethora of savings frees China from the trap that long hampered the growth of emergent countries, especially in Latin America: a shortage of currency.

Chinese saving causes perplexity among economists, just as Japanese saving once did. Why don't the Chinese want to consume more? The answer doesn't seem to relate to some supposed frugality, since their standards of consumption are rapidly approaching those of the West. Already there are 94 color TVs and 46 refrigerators for every 100 households. Their eating habits are also being modified and approaching those of the West. McDonald's opens 100 new branches in China per year. The Chinese go crazy for major foreign brands. In 2005 the advertising agency Ernst & Young published a report predicting that in 2015 the Chinese will account for one-third of the worldwide demand for luxury items, on a par with Japan and far ahead of other countries. Also on the model of Japan, armies of Chinese are engaging in long-distance tourism. A hundred million Chinese tourists are expected to go abroad in 2013, as opposed to 30 million today.[13]

Chinese savings do not result, then, from a particular difficulty the country might have in embracing Western consumer society. The paradox is the reverse. The speed with which Chinese standards of consumption have approached those of the West is astonishing. But how can we understand their savings level of 50 percent? There are two explanatory factors. First, any economy enjoying strong growth tends to generate high rates of savings. And when revenues grow by 10 percent a year, it takes time for the norms of consumption to adjust to the new possibilities. Second, profit rates are considerable and outstrip investment capabilities. These high profits reflect the chronic weakness of salaries.

The new reserve army

China has seen both a spectacular decrease in its number of poor (defined on the basis of a minimum of a dollar a day) and a spectacular increase in inequality.[14] The decrease in the number of poor still owes much to the measures taken at first to liberalize agricultural production. The industrialization that followed multiplied the gap between the richest 10 percent and the poorest 10 percent fourfold, with the latter's level of remuneration remaining stagnant—and three-fourths of the poorest 10 percent of the Chinese population are peasants.

The balance between town and country relies on a particularly perverse system, that of migrant workers. In the classical scheme of rural exodus that once prevailed, especially in Europe, peasants left the countryside to go to cities to settle permanently. The first few generations suffered, but their children ended up integrating into the urban civilization. The Chinese scheme was conceived in such a way that migrants are almost forced to "return to the country" to start a family. It relies on a system that assigns each person a place of residence: that of one's mother. This iron rule determines one's right of access to public benefits. For example, children can benefit from public schooling or health care only in the official *houkou* of the parents. Thus it is nearly impossible for a "migrant worker"—meaning a worker residing outside his assigned zone—to start a family.[15]

Today in China there are some 130 million migrant workers, who make up nearly one-fourth of the urban workforce. Among migrants, only one-eighth of the children attend school. An analogy between these migrant workers and the "industrial reserve army"— as Marx conceived of the proletariat, obliged to do all the worst-paid work—comes immediately to mind. The *houkou* is a perverse means of maintaining in semi-legality a workforce of people who are like immigrants in their own country. This system creates a dualism in the Chinese population that is a heresy from the economic standpoint and a mark of cynicism in the political realm.

From an economic standpoint, this system is particularly ineffective. The professional life cycle of migrant workers is truncated. Going back home to raise families, they scarcely work any longer. As such, there is an "earning gap" for the whole country, comparable to what France is suffering when it is incapable of making those over 55 years of age work any longer. Their children must then start again learning to lead an urban life, painfully inserting themselves into the interstices of society. The promotion of peasants into an urban middle class is blocked.

From a political standpoint, the advantage of the system was still apparent during the crisis of 2008. The first victims of the slow-down, promptly repatriated to their territories of origin, were the migrant workers, a class of temporary workers without benefits and the first to be fired. In the context of this crisis, *houkou* can be inter-preted as a baroque and cruel system that is costly from the stand-point of long-term growth but effective in periods of social tension, allowing those at risk to be sent far away from the centers.

"China worries me"

One of the elements of China's rediscovered dynamism is also one of its weaknesses: rivalry among the provinces. David Landes explained that, ironically, if China had remained at the stage of the seven king-doms that prevailed before the formation of the Han Empire in the third century BCE, it would no doubt have fared better than under the imperial regime, for it would have benefited from the same stimulus as European nations did. Today the seven kingdoms are back in a new guise. The Chinese provinces benefit from a new autonomy. They are directed by a class of politicians that the Sinolo-gist Jean-Luc Domenach calls, in his 2008 book *La Chine m'inquiète*, a new plutocracy whose principal motive is personal enrichment. But in contrast with corrupt states whose elites curb any economic dynamism, this corruption has remained a growth factor. Provincial authorities vie to attract foreign investment, playing on their com-parative advantages with respect to infrastructures, and by doing so they stimulate overall investment. The sharp rivalry among regions plays a role akin to that among European nation-states in the sixteenth century.

The complex balance between central power and regional powers is one of the major uncertainties of the current dynamic. A sometimes subtle, sometimes brutal game is set up between the two power sources. The centralized authority in Beijing tries to keep the upper hand, which sometimes takes the form of a call to order in the face of local drifts, with struggle against corruption one of the favorite themes of central intervention. This regional maneuver opens a narrow channel into which defenders of the law move—the "barefoot lawyers" who are slowly spreading the idea of human rights in Chinese society, often at the risk of their own freedom. But the central authority also uses a more dangerous lever: flattering nationalist impulses in the country. Jean-Luc Domenach comments on how Chinese authorities manipulate anti-Japanese resentment among the common people. He adds that "they do so in case things don't work out," i.e., in case they have to find a scapegoat for a possible failure. In China today, as in Europe yesterday, nationalism is a weapon that solders together a society in transition. Here we cannot resist a comparison to Germany at the beginning of the twentieth century. Germany was torn between Prussian power (reincarnated in China by the Chinse Communist Party) and the rising bourgeoisie (in China, businessmen and the plutocracy).

The Olympic Games were part of the policy of flattering Chinese nationalism. However, China's leaders nearly committed the same error that the Soviet authorities made when the Olympics were held in Moscow in 1980. You cannot let the Western press run around a country with impunity without arousing a domestic demand for political expression, of which Tibet gave the example in the Chinese case. Democratization and the demand for a free press do not derive from prosperity as such, but from openness to the world, to images and ideas. This is the other theater of globalization—perhaps the more important one.

INDIA'S AWAKENING

The question that tormented Joseph Needham—why China did not give birth to a Galileo or a Newton—is not posed in the same terms in the Indian case. Despite advances in mathematics (the invention of negative numbers), India's prowess in technical domains wasn't as spectacular as China's. Indian agriculture is certainly varied, including rice, wheat, millet, sugarcane, oil, cotton, silk, and jute. This formidable agricultural wealth wasn't carried forward by particularly advanced technical skill, however. Indians relied on intensive work techniques rather than on subtle technologies. The apparent splendor of the Mogul Dynasty (1526–1858) owes much more to the extraordinary inequality that overtook Indian society than to prosperity itself. To extend the parallel with Europe, India rather incarnates the destiny of Eastern Europe (east of the Elbe), where work long remained similarly subject to a profoundly inegalitarian system.

India's independence, achieved in 1947, did not change the basic traits of the society from one day to the next. Jawaharlal Nehru gave one of the most beautiful speeches on human liberty, but he spoke in English, the language of the colonizer, spoken by only a minority of Indians. This anecdote underlines the difficulty of newly independent countries trying to be free of both the codes of colonization and their own heritage of inequality. Nehru died in 1964 and was succeeded two years later by his daughter Indira Gandhi, who remained in power from 1966 to 1977. Thus the Nehru–Gandhi era lasted nearly 30 years, during which the average annual growth in per capita income was 0.7 percent per year. This was better than before, when the numbers had been, on average, negative. In 1946 the per capita income of an Indian was lower than in 1913. But the result obtained after independence remained quite weak in comparison with the figures achieved in Japan or South Korea. Great poverty remained, touching 55 percent of the population.

Throughout this period, growth was hindered by the "License Raj," an omnipresent administrative system that required authorization at almost all levels of the production chain. Set up by Nehru almost from the moment of independence, the system closed India to the rest of the world in economic matters. But the most spectacular failure of this system would be in the political realm. Bureaucratic organization favors a system in which corruption thrives; any request for permission entails a payoff to the functionary who is responsible for granting it. In 2005, Transparency International ranked India 98th on the list of nations struggling against corruption.

One of the paradoxical effects of this strategy is visible today. India certainly lost time by deferring its entry into the world, but when openness did arrive it already possessed the "primitive accumulation" of talents that is now its strength. Its success in the information and pharmaceuticals sectors followed on the failures of the strategy of aiming to develop those sectors by cutting them off from the rest of the world. Whereas once chemists and engineers were obliged to reinvent everything, now the previously protected sectors possess a formidable reserve of skills with which to meet the challenges of openness.

The attitude of India's leaders toward commercial openness would change abruptly. After her triumphal reelection in January 1980, Indira Gandhi—probably piqued by the changes underway in China—explored other avenues. The production quotas given to small businesses were relaxed, and restrictions on the import of equipment were timidly lifted. In Gandhi's first year in power, tariff duties on manufacturing equipment were reduced by half.

Almost imperceptibly, without appearing to be more favorable to the market, Indira Gandhi became more "pro-business," to use Dani Rodrik's useful phrase. India had several great industrial dynasties that emerged around the second half of the nineteenth century, such as Ambani, Mittal, Tata—the latter of which alone controlled 3 percent of India's GDP. It was to the founder of the Tata dynasty that Indians owed the construction of the Taj Mahal Hotel in 1903. That hotel was built as an answer to an insult that one of the Tata dynasty's founders suffered when he was forbidden access to the Watson Hotel, a British-only establishment situated opposite the site of the new hotel. Fearing an untimely intrusion of political power into their affairs, India's industrial dynasties nevertheless remained cautious about their own development. The government's change in policy was opening the doors to a more aggressive strategy.

When Indira Gandhi was assassinated in 1984 by her Sikh bodyguards, her son Rajiv pursued her policy. When he was assassinated in 1991, the economy was still in a fragile state. The balance-of-payments deficit, the budgetary deficit, and inflation all threatened economic growth. But with the arrival of a new team directed by Narasimha Rao and Manmohar Singh the break with the past became irreversible.

The journalist David Smith compares the duo of Rao and Singh to Deng Xiaoping in China.[16] Rao was a veteran of the Congress Party, the Gandhi party. Manmohar Singh was a Cambridge-educated economist and a former governor of the Central Bank. In a few months, they lowered customs tariffs nearly 100 percent on average (and key ones by 355 percent) to an average of 25–30 percent. The rupee was devalued by 22 percent in relation to the dollar in order to stimulate exports. A new policy with regard to foreign investment was also launched.[17] On July 24, 1991, Singh spoke passionately to the national assembly, quoting Victor Hugo to the effect that there is nothing so powerful in the world as an idea whose hour has come. His Statement of Industrial Policy was also compared to Lenin's New Economic Policy, established to restart the Soviet economy in the 1920s.

Despite a revival of growth that might have spelled reelection for the Congress Party team, it was the opposition party, the Bharatiya Jana Party, that carried the 1998 elections. The BJP, a Hindu nationalist party, was very critical of economic liberalization and of globalization, and it sharpened tensions with the Muslims. In the state of Gujarat, on the border with Pakistan, it organized anti-Muslim pogroms in 1992 that left indelible scars on relations between the two communities. After the parliamentary victory of the BJP, it seemed uncertain that the reforms would endure, but to general surprise the BJP carried on with the previous policy. And when, five years later, the Congress Party (directed by Sonia, Rajiv's widow, who was of Italian origin) came back to power, Singh, who had been Minister of Finance under Rao, became prime minister. India, whose growth rate then hovered just below 10 percent a year, seems to have accomplished its own Asiatic tiger's leap.

Vulnerable India

Despite its high growth rates, India remains poor, undermined by its inequalities and by the weight of tradition that hampered social ascension for the lower classes. According to the consulting firm McKinsey & Company, India could be sliced into four categories: a small elite of 1.2 million very rich households, 40 million medium-income households that could hope to reach the norms of Western consumption, 110 million households trying to live on an annual income ranting from $1,500 to $4,000 a year (just above the poverty line), and the mass of the truly poverty-stricken (who still form a majority). Forty percent of children are suffering from malnutrition, a higher percentage than in Africa. How could a country that describes itself as the largest democracy in the world allow such chasms of inequality? Let us return to this disturbing question by following Christophe Jaffrelot's in-depth study.[18]

First of all, India indeed respects most of the criteria that enable it to claim the title of "largest democracy in the world." With the sole exception of the state of emergency decreed by Indira Gandhi in 1977–1979 (after which she lost the elections), the democratic process has always been scrupulously respected. The media are free, never sparing criticism of the current government. Starting in the 1980s, alternation of parties became the rule, with the Congress Party (Nehru's) yielding power to a coalition dominated by the socialist-inspired Janata Dal (People's Party). Then it was the turn of the BJP, the anti-Muslim party of the right. In 2004 the BJP ceded power to the Congress Party.

Despite firm principles, India has had great difficulty moving from a formal democracy to a social democracy that aims to really reduce inequalities. Castes have remained an invisible barrier to social mobility. The Congress Party itself is essentially a party of the high castes, symbolized by the Brahmins. Bhinrao Ambedkar, an untouchable, made an inspired criticism of this implausible system, which is founded, he says, "on a rising ladder of reverence and a falling ladder of contempt"—everyone despises someone who is lower and aspires to climb higher, and no one ever questions the ladder itself.

This caste system establishes a division of labor that is reproduced from one generation to the next. Gandhi, who actually remained respectful of this system, even saw it as "a healthy division of labor founded on birth," adding: "I think that in the same way as each person inherits a certain physical appearance [from his parents] each also inherits from his progenitors certain characteristics and certain particular qualities, and to admit that enables keeping one's energy."

Congress has remained a "catch-all" party, dominated nationally by progressives who do not think that caste is a useful social category and locally by notables who desire to preserve their interests and their positions. The party has tried to organize a "coalition of extremes" by enrolling untouchables. But under vigilant pressure from notables, its program has proved much more conservative than its rhetoric, especially in the realms of agrarian reform and access to education. The Communists, because they talk about classes and not castes, have gradually lost ground and are incapable of mobilizing the disadvantaged castes that are seeking emancipation.

Nevertheless, change has occurred over the years. Positive discrimination, linked to caste membership rather than to solely socioeconomic criteria, was introduced. On December 20, 1978, Prime Minister Moraji Desai decided to appoint a commission to analyze the issue of disadvantaged castes, those designated as "other backward castes" (OBC) to distinguish them from the untouchables. The Mandal Commission concluded in favor of positive discrimination, arguing that "treating persons suffering from inequalities as equals amounts to perpetuating inequality." And the rising power of the lower castes began then. Coming to power in 1989, the Janata Dal party, led by V. P. Singh, decided that "the government would take all necessary measures for the implementation of the Mandal Commission's recommendations."

The two parties led by the upper castes, Congress and the BJP, have tried to adapt to the Mandal Report by opening posts to disadvantaged castes and to *dalits* (untouchables). The BJP also tried to attract the lower castes by playing on the anti-Muslim discourse, which enabled it to win elections—but the recipe did not last long, for it lost the subsequent ones. Political power had begun to change hands. The untouchables did free themselves from the Congress Party, carrying one of their own, K. R. Narayanan, to the presidency of the republic.

The expected explosion of violence feared by Gandhi did not take place. Brahmins did begin a hunger strike after the publication of the Mandal Report, but tension quickly subsided. According to Jaffrelot, this relative calm relates in part to the fact that at the very moment when new quotas were assigned to benefit lower castes in the public sector, the higher ones could fall back on a private sector that had become very attractive thanks to new economic growth. A new sharing of tasks was silently taking effect. The elites were turning to the economy, leaving political power to the lower strata. The journey

---

that had led the Western elites to pass "from political passions to economic interest" may be occurring today in India. The cocktail seems to work for the time being, but remains fragile. Positive discrimination founded on castes is a good thing in the short term. But it runs the risk of each person being shut in the prison of his or her birth.

12

The End of History and the West

The Tragedy of Weak Nations

The entry of India and China into the game of world capitalism is inseparable from another major episode: the disappearance of the USSR. As its crisis was becoming patent, the USSR, which had adhered to the idea of state socialism, gradually changed its strategy. The fall of the Berlin Wall made some think that the world had reached (in a term borrowed from Hegel and taken up by Francis Fukuyama) "the end of history."[19] According to that theory, all countries now tended toward the same destination: the market economy and representative democracy. The universal peace dreamed of by Kant had finally become a real possibility.

However, on September 11, 2001, the attack on the twin towers of the World Trade Center opened the twenty-first century just as noisily as the fall of the Berlin Wall on November 9, 1989 has closed the twentieth. Contrary to the optimistic thesis defended by

Fukuyama, Samuel Huntington's thesis of a "clash of civilizations" appeared to be more of a premonition.[20] For Huntington, the East and the West will never converge; the great Eastern civilizations will tend more to reconstitute their lost power than to construct a democratic and peaceful world. The upshot of Huntington's "realist policy" is to let each country cultivate its own garden if one wants to avoid a new world war.

How to choose between Fukuyama and Huntington? Do civilizations converge toward a single model, that of a "market democracy," or does each pursue a singular trajectory? It is tempting to answer "Neither." Seeing emerging countries today taking the path that was Europe's in the course of the last five centuries suggests a third hypothesis: a return of the risks that Europe had to confront. And peaceful resolution is only one of the possibilities open today. The other is a repetition of the same sequence of wars and upheavals.[21]

The market and democracy

The massacres in Yugoslavia and Rwanda and the anti-Muslim pogroms in India's Gujarat region rapidly squelched any hope of the universal peace that was anticipated when the Berlin Wall came down. As Arjun Appadurai says, this violence has manifested "a surplus of rage, an excess of hatred that produces untold forms of degradation and violation, both to the body and the being of the victim: maimed and tortured bodies, burned and raped persons, disemboweled women, hacked and amputated children, sexual humiliation of every type."[22]

In her book *The World on Fire*, Amy Chua, a lawyer of Chinese-Philippine origin, gives a poignant personal account of the murder of her aunt Leon by her Filipino chauffeur in 1994.[23] The motive selected by the police to characterize the murder was "vengeance." Amy Chua's family belonged to the prosperous minority of Chinese immigrants; to Filipinos, she represented 1 percent of the population and 60 percent of the wealth. In Indonesia, the figures are nearly equivalent; as in the Philippines, the Chinese dominate business and industry. In 1998 in Jakarta, furious crowds burned and pillaged hundreds of Chinese houses and shops, causing more than 2,000 deaths. "One who survived—a fourteen-year-old Chinese girl—later committed suicide by taking rat poison. She had been gang-raped and genitally mutilated in front of her parents."[24]

Amy Chua's book results from traumatizing experience. Everywhere economically dominant minorities exist, she explains, the mixture of a market and democracy forms an explosive cocktail. "The competition for votes fosters the emergence of demagogues who scapegoat the resented minority and foment active ethnonationalist movements demanding that the country's wealth and identity be reclaimed by the 'true owners of the nation.'"[25]

Amy Chua emphasizes the problem of rich minorities, but the problem is the same when the minorities are poor. As Appadurai says, when they are designated to suffer popular violence, minorities are always guilty. "When they are wealthy, they raise the specter of elite globalization working as its pariah mediators. And when they are poor, they are the convenient symbols of the failure of many forms of development and welfare."[26] Poor minorities suffer twice; cultural exclusion is compounded by economic exclusion. In Mexico, for example, 81 percent of the indigenous people have an income below the poverty threshold, as opposed to 18 percent of the general population. In Nepal, the mortality rate of children less than 5 years of age in the lower castes exceeds 17 percent, while it is only about 7 percent for the Newars and the Brahmins. Thirty percent of Roma (gypsy) children in Serbia-Montenegro never go to primary school. Black men and children in São Paolo earn only half the salaries of whites. Many such examples can be cited, all of them illustrating the vicious circle of stigmatization and economic exclusion.

According to *Cultural Liberty in Today's Diverse World*, a report published by the UN Development Program in 2004, nearly a billion individuals belong to groups that are victims of one or another form of exclusion (ethnic, religious, or more generally "cultural"). More than 150 countries have minority groups representing at least 10 percent of their population; in 100 countries, these minorities constitute more than 25 percent of the population. The UN report makes a passionate appeal for the defense of cultural freedom: "People want the freedom to practice their religion openly, to speak their language, to celebrate their ethnic or religious heritage without fear of ridicule or punishment or diminished opportunity."

This aspiration for recognition of their rights, alas, was one of the elements that triggered the tragedies of the 1990s. As Appadurai says, the promise of democracy that followed the fall of the Berlin Wall incited exploited minorities to demand protection of their cultural rights. According to him, it was this explosive cocktail that erupted in the 1990s.

Starting from the other end of society, Appadurai's reasoning converges with that of Amy Chua. The marriage between democracy and the market economy is not always a brilliant one. In order to succeed, the two must first understand each other and agree with each other. This is the problem of forming a nation.

The nation

As Hannah Arendt says, summarizing her long study of *The Origins of Totalitarianism*, the nation is the Achilles' heel of modern societies. Ideally, the nation is a political community that abolishes differences between its members by conferring on them equal rights and duties.[27] But when the state is in crisis, or quite simply in difficulty, the nation is reduced to the fiction of its ethnic purity. And then all manner of terrible things become possible. As the British historian Ian Kershaw has shown, Nazism was nourished by a "millenarian and pseudo-religious vision of 'national revival,' incarnated in the idea of 'national community' (*Volksgemeinschaft*), advocating moving beyond political and religious divisions and classes through the creation of a new ethnic identity founded on the 'true' German values."[28]

Arendt and Kershaw are trying to understand the origins of Nazism, but their statements apply universally. René Girard has perfectly described how, in a society that can no longer understand itself, violence against "undesirable" minorities enables members of the majority to know who they are by default. As Girard shows, it is not the minorities who are the triggers of violence, but the exact opposite.[29]

In the poorest regions in the world, in Africa especially, many countries simply haven't reached the point at which a monopoly on violence is recognized as belonging to the state. As the economist Paul Collier says in *The Bottom Billion* (2007), the reference that enables us to understand their destiny is to Europe in the fourteenth century, when plague, war, and famine were elements of everyday life.[30] In countries ravaged by civil wars—a phenomenon that Collier characterizes as "development in reverse"—the construction of

a modern state that replaces feudalism and pacifies its domestic space
has not yet begun. These countries lack the long work of eradicating
violence that was effected in Europe over several centuries.

The divergent trajectories of states born after European colonization also illuminates this essential question. What difference is
there between Mexico and the United States, or between South
Africa and New Zealand? Why are some poor and tardy in reaching democracy, and others prosperous and democratic? In answer to
these questions, Daron Acemoglu, Simon Johnson, and James Robinson have offered an astonishing theory that René Girard would not
dispute.[31] According to their analysis, it is simple. Countries in which
Europeans exterminated the "Indians" are rich today; inversely,
countries in which the colonizers remained in the minority are poor.
Acemoglu and his co-authors show that there is a very significant
statistical link between the morbidity of those colonized and current
wealth. How do they explain this surprising result?

Their argument has nothing to do with any presumed superiority of Europeans over local peoples; another mechanism is at
work. Where the Europeans remained a minority, they didn't try to
manufacture a modern state accountable for the security of persons
and private property. What interested them was exploiting the local
peoples, precisely out of contempt for these rights. Inversely, where
whites "remained among themselves," they imported (keys in hand)
the institutions of their country of origin, England, thereby hasten-
ing the formation of a modern state.

These observations testify to an underlying phenomenon.
Modern economic growth needs to rely on the modern framework
of nation-states. In order to produce wealth, it needs, in nearly equal

shares, capital (machines), human capital (education, public health), and effective institutions (organized markets and rule of law). But human capital and institutions are produced by the state; they constitute what economists call the social infrastructures of the nation. They depend on the fact that the state is the guarantor of the "public good," without which individual success is impossible. For example, Japan's success, copied everywhere in Asia, relates precisely to that country's capacity to give itself fundamental public goods: schools, public health, justice, territory. These are the factors that remain tragically absent from the countries on the periphery of globalization—those whom Paul Collier characterizes as "the billion below," which are always caught in a demographic trap, and whose population will reach 2 billion in 2050.

Collier describes the situation in the poorest countries as a poverty trap. A weak state prevents economic development, and in turn poverty restrains the emergence of a strong state.

This political and economic trap is an example that illustrates a more general rule. Economics and politics are interlinked, but by necessity more than by real harmony. An economy in decline fatally signals the decadence of the political regime it supports, just as a publicly weak state prevents economic development. Similarly but inversely, a growing economy helps the state achieve its projects, whether expansionist or socially beneficial, and a strong state, provided that it is not too threatening, is a factor in growth. But nothing is fixed immutably. The most striking phenomenon of the nascent twenty-first century—the conversion of India and China to world capitalism—was produced without any notable institutional rupture with the past. Some reforms sufficed to revive the long-stifled dynamism of those societies and to put them on the path to rapid growth.[32] But nothing guarantees that this conversion will last. Prudence is required about the duration of these transformations. As Albert Hirschman says in *The Passions and the Interests*, rather than assuming that economic development ineluctably entails political development, it is better to recognize that "the political impact of economic development is essentially ambivalent, and its effect works simultaneously in both directions," shaken by phases of expansion and phases of contraction.[33]

The Critique of the West

Let us return to Samuel Huntington's thesis that the old civilizations of the world are by no means converging, and that underneath the shared veil of consumer society there are systems of antagonistic values that threaten to confront each other. Among the many critiques of this theory, one of the most convincing was formulated by those who insisted that the idea of the East's rejecting of Western values wasn't very original, having been formulated often in the West itself. As Ian Buruma and Avishai Margalit brilliantly show in their book *Occidentalism*, this criticism traversed Europe throughout the nineteenth century and the first half of the twentieth.[34] Almost from the start, the vision of human history proposed by the Enlightenment was criticized by German Romanticism. Whereas the Enlightenment thinkers had an optimistic vision of human history, which they saw as a linear progression toward a better and more rational world, the Romantics offered a different approach, guided by a new sequence—that of "innocence, the fall, and redemption." In the nineteenth century, the decline of the West became a major theme of Western literature.

The Romantic critique of the modern world targeted the pretension of science to govern people, arguing that science was incapable of understanding the suffering of the human soul and denouncing it as a mode of thought without wisdom. Science created a dehumanized world, a world disenchanted by the relegation of religion to the rank of superstition. Turgenev caricatured his hero Bazarov in *Fathers and Sons* as a fanatic adept of scientism, a convinced utilitarian. Flaubert did the same with the pharmacist Homais in *Madame Bovary*.

In another critique of the modern world, Marx reproached the bourgeoisie for having "drowned heroism in the icy waters of selfish calculation." What Sombart, Oswald, Spengler, Jünger, and other German intellectuals would despise the most was bourgeois cowardice, which consisted of clinging to life and not wanting to die for ideas. Sombart used the term *Konfortismus* to describe this bourgeois mentality, and Heidegger thought *Amerikanismus* was emptying the European soul. The image of a complacent bourgeois became that of a coward, the opposite of a hero ready to sacrifice his life. The West was mediocre because it gave each person the possibility of being mediocre, according to the German nationalist writer Arthur Moeller van der Bruch. The West was a threat because it diminished the value of any utopia.

In Germany, the resentment felt toward France also broke into the open. According to Isaiah Berlin, the Romantic movement was partially an anti-French reaction. National sensitivity had been wounded by the conviction that the nation had been horribly humiliated by the Napoleonic armies. The enthusiasm of Fredrick the Great in the eighteenth century for French culture, his mania to import everything from France, merely aggravated German resentment.

The case of Frederic II is not isolated. Rulers often wanted to import the Western model, before discovering that their people would not follow. In Russia, Peter the Great required the landed nobility, the *boyards*, to shave their beards. He then required priests to give sermons on the virtues of reason. Kemal Ataturk, who came to power in Turkey in 1923, wanted to adopt Western technologies and codes in matters of dress and hair. He forbade the veil, as the Shah of Iran would also do. In the cities, the Shah sent the army on patrols to force women to take off their veils, sometimes under threat, and forced religious dignitaries to remove their turbans.[35]

The renewal of political Islam can be interpreted as a consequence of this modernization at a forced pace by totalitarian regimes. The Islamist revolutionary movement would never have seen the light of day without the brutal secularism of Reza Shah Pahlavi or the failed experiments in socialism in Egypt, Syria, and Algeria. As Albert Memmi would explain in a prescient book written in 1957 that perfectly anticipated this evolution, Middle Eastern dictatorships left their peoples only religion as a site of contestation, a space that was quickly occupied.[36]

Political Islamism is the expression of a rejection that by no means signifies "the clash of civilizations." All civilizations (led by the West) have fed and continue to feed an opposition to modernization. In Japan of the Meiji era, at the end of the nineteenth century, the samurais traded their kimonos for frock coats and top hats. They made a duty of destroying Buddhist temples and of transforming their country in the name of Progress, Science, and Enlightenment. But during that era, Japanese peasants would settle in the cities in miserable conditions worthy of Dickens, where, according to Buruma and Margalit, "they sometimes had to sell their sisters to the brothels of the big cities." In Japan, as in Germany, resentment of the intrusion of the modern world nourished the rise of extremists and would feed World War II.

The eternal return of violence

European history shows that we should not wait for the transition from the rural world to the industrial world to take place in the cozy comfort of democracy and the market economy. Quite often, it is violence—when it reaches its paroxysm—that is the vector of this transition.

In Europe, violence began to recede after the bloodshed of the Wars of Religion in the sixteenth and seventeenth centuries. It was after the atrocities committed during the Thirty Years War (which ended in 1648) that the state began to acquire a monopoly on legitimate violence. But the first turning point was only a stage. The European case shows the sinuous paths that violence can take; when it ebbs on one front, it shifts to another one. Throughout the nineteenth century, as attacks became confined to persons or property, violence migrated to private space, that of conjugal violence. Men who had become less aggressive toward other men now more often attacked women and children. Sexual abuse of minors grew constantly, inversely to general criminality. Now excluded from public space, violence shifted to homes. And the French courts long remained understanding toward those who killed out of "love, jealousy, or confusion." Not until the 1880s were the growing reports of the rape of little girls, of incest, and of torture of minors acted upon.

Eventually, the only legitimate violence at the disposal of society is that of war. Muchembled concludes that "at the start of the

---

twentieth century, it was a striking paradox that violence had become unacceptable for those who thought they were civilized, while the terrible human butchery of 1914–1918 was being prepared. Would this be a formidable return of the repressed?"[37]

According to Muchembled, there still exists a third zone where violence can take hold, a zone between private violence and public violence: that of the imaginary. As urban delinquency receded, more and more European metropolises were gripped by fear of the "dangerous classes." As violence decreased, fear was exacerbated. Reading crime novels became a way of exorcizing anguish. Beginning in the middle of the eighteenth century, murderers and thieves composed an "army of dark shadows" that occupied the nightmares and reading material of the new city audience. Blood sold paper and ink. Figures who incarnated evil and death, like Tenebras and Zigomar, were tracked by Sherlock Holmes and his French counterpart, Rouletabille. Fantomas, the "evil genius," began his career in 1911. In the whole Fantomas series (which lasted until 1963), there are not just a few detailed attacks, woundings, kidnappings, imprisonments, and homicides for villainous motives like pride or vengeance—in all, there are 552 such crimes.

These different levels of violence are at work today, simultaneously, all over the world. Violence against Tutsis, Bosnians, the Muslims of Gujarat, and other groups translate the pathologies of disturbed nations and draw their force from the mechanisms described by René Girard. One has to kill the other to exist oneself and, what is more, to exist as a member of a community, in the image of the violence produced during the European wars of religion.

To this risk of the recrudescence of hate crimes, we must add those born of the most ordinary risks of legitimate violence: those of states against other states. The list of hot spots where this phenomenon is obvious includes the border between India and Pakistan, the sea that separates China and Japan, and the border between Russia and Georgia. There still are conflicts between an aggressive nation (often an old empire) and its neighbors, whose independence aggravates the old master because it imperils its domestic equilibrium.

The third stage of violence is that of the imaginary—today, the postmodern violence of horror films and video games, now found everywhere but principally in the rich countries. This is the violence of the twenty-first century, of which the September 11 attack can be taken as an example. Relayed by cameras all over the world, it was aimed at the collective imagination much more than at the material power of the United States. The Tenebras and Zigomars have changed name and tone, but the sought-after effect remains the same.

13

The Ecological Crash

The Crowded Planet

The industrialization of the whole world upsets the rules that prevailed when industrialization was limited to Western countries and Japan. A new threat hovers over nations, weighing on the planet itself, the last common good. This is the terrain onto which the danger of collective suicide has now been displaced.

The emerging countries take paths patterned after those of the West, for they intend to profit in their turn from the promises of modern economic growth. On average, this process of convergence is indeed underway, especially in Asia. Jeffrey Sachs provides many insightful figures in his book *Commonwealth*. Extrapolating from current tendencies, the emergent countries could reach between now and 2050 an average level of development of $40,000 per capita, or about the level of the United States in 2005. Such growth would enable emergent countries to multiply their per capita income by 4.

PART III

Supposing that the income of rich countries also continues to increase at the current rates, then poor countries will go from an average ratio gap of 1:15 to a ratio of 1:2.5. Taking into account the rise in world population (which should swell from 6 billion to 9 billion people), the wealth wrought out of the earth would then be multiplied by a factor of 6, from $70 trillion in 2005 to $420 trillion in 2050. However, such is also the increase in the ecological borrowing that humankind will inflict on the planet.[38]

Nothing will prepare the earth for such an upheaval. Until the eighteenth century, humankind depended on the sun (and to a lesser extent on water and wind) as energy sources. Then everything changed. The chemist Paul Crutzen summarized the current evolution as the emergence of the "Anthropocene," the shift from a world dominated by nature to a world dominated by humans. One figure summarizes the meaning of this term. At the time agricultural developed, human beings, their flocks, and their domesticated animals accounted for less than 0.1 percent of all vertebrates. Today, they account for 98 percent.

Globalization marks a quantum leap in the scale of problems created by humans. The single fact of Chinese growth upsets the balance between supply and demand of natural resources. For the five basic raw materials (grains, meat, petroleum, coal, and steel), China comes out ahead four times in world consumption; the single exception (for the time being) is petroleum consumption, in which it remains outstripped by the United States. China in 2005 consumed 380 million tons of cereals, the United States 260 million tons. China was ahead of the United States in consumption of wheat and rice, and behind it only in corn. Chinese consumption of steel is nearly twice American consumption (258 million tons versus 104). In the realm of modern consumer goods, China is in first place for cell phones, televisions, and refrigerators. The United States remains the leading consumer of cars and computers—but not for long.

If China sticks to American habits of consumption, by 2030 it may consume two-thirds of the level of the world's current production of grain. If China catches up to the US in consumption of paper, it will consume 305 billion tons—enough to gobble up all the planet's forests. As Lester Brown puts it, "The Western economic model . . . will not work for China's 1.45 billion in 2031." Nor could the Western model be applicable to India, whose population will exceed China's by that date.[39]

If the Chinese someday possess, on the American model, three vehicles for every four inhabitants, roads and parking facilities will exceed the space today devoted to growing rice.[40] China will then consume 99 million barrels of oil per day. The world currently produces 84 million barrels a day, and it will not be long before that declines. Although the proven oil reserves doubled between 1980 and 2000, that rate has tended to decrease since then, with discoveries of new fields now lower than annual production.[41] Among the 23 producing countries, 15 have already reached their "production peak"—their annual production has already begun to decline.

Global warming

Global warming is the most famous and most worrying manifestation of the effects of industrialization on the planet. Eleven of the twelve hottest years ever recorded were between 1995 and 2006. This heating is associated with a significant rise in periods of drought, in extreme hurricanes such as Katrina (which swamped

---

New Orleans), and in heat waves like the one that caused the death of 38,000 people in Europe in 2003. The list of consequences of warming is long: rising sea levels, extinction of polar bears and other species, transmission of illnesses to certain regions (such as the high African plains) that formerly were protected from them by a temperate climate, increased desertification, increased scarcity of available water, the threat of accelerated melting of glaciers and of floods. All these upheavals result from global warming, itself linked to emissions of greenhouse gases.

Greenhouse gases (CO_2, water vapor, methane) let through the ultraviolet (high-frequency) light that is emitted by the sun, which traverses the atmosphere and heats the Earth.[42] But they block the infrared (low-frequency) rays that are emitted by the Earth. Thus, they let through solar radiation, but trap the heat that results from it, as in a greenhouse.

Deforestation and combustion of fossil fuels have increased the concentration of CO_2 in the atmosphere from 280 parts per million (ppm) at the start of the industrial era to 390 ppm in 2010. Since 1850, the temperature has increased on average by 0.8°C. Even if today we completely stopped the emission of CO_2 the temperature would still continue to increase by 1.0°C, because the warming of the oceans is delayed.

The implications of global warming were described in detail in reports commissioned by the British government (the Stern Report) and by the Inter-Governmental Panel on Climate Change (IPCC).[43] According to these reports, if one sticks to extrapolating from past tendencies, the concentration of CO_2 will increase from 390 ppm to 560 ppm by the end of the twenty-first century. A doubling of CO_2 is considered as the extreme limit of acceptable risk; beyond this threshold, all kinds of disturbances are possible. Moreover, the probable evolution could be much more rapid than what results from simple extrapolation. The entry of China and India into the industrial world threatens reaching the critical threshold of 560 ppm not at the *end* of the twenty-first century, but already by 2050. Moreover, a complex array of factors will be added to the new emissions of CO_2. The warming of oceans might also free the CO_2 and methane that today are dissolved in them. The melting of glaciers also reduces the reflection of sunlight and so directly contributes to warming.

Other curses

The disappearance of species is another aspect of Anthropocene. Ecologists warn about what they call the sixth great extinction of species. The five first episodes were due to the disruptions induced by variations in planetary orbit, by volcanic eruptions, or by asteroid impacts. In the most recent episode, nearly one-fourth of bird species disappeared from the planet in the course of the last two millennia. Two-thirds of the main fisheries are already "totally exploited, over-exploited, or on the way to disappearing."

Water is another great problem of the twenty-first century. The ecology of the first agricultural societies was often linked to the existence of a river—the Nile, the Tigris, the Euphrates, the Ganges, the Yangtse. The proximity of rivers enables irrigating the soil, and profiting from trees for heat and lodging. A number of these great rivers today no longer reach the sea, or else see their flow dramatically reduced in the summertime. The Nile and the Ganges are reduced to a trickle during the dry seasons. The flow of the Nile is practically nil when the river reaches the Mediterranean. If Sudan and Ethiopia decided to increase their consumption, a conflict with Egypt would be inevitable. The same problem is posed by the Tigris and the Euphrates. Large dams constructed in Turkey and in Iraq have reduced the flow of the ancient "fertile crescent," contributing to the destruction of 90 percent of the once-vast humid zone that secured the wealth of the delta region between the two rivers.

Water goes through a natural cycle of evaporation and condensation, or else is obtained from fossil layers buried in the ground. But the fossil resources are quickly being exhausted. A crushing majority of the 3 billion persons who will be born between now and 2050 will live in countries where such layers are overexploited. Many villages of northwest India already have been abandoned. Millions of villagers from the north and the west of China, and from certain regions of Mexico, are being pushed into exile by a lack of water. In China, according to Lester Brown, "the water table under the North China Plain, which produces over half of that country's wheat and a third of its corn, is falling faster than earlier reported." The declines in China's wheat and rice crops are directly linked to this growing scarcity of water.

In India, too, the aquifers are falling rapidly—in northern Gujarat, by 20 meters per year. According to Lester Brown, "when the balloon bursts, untold anarchy will be the lot of rural India."[44] India will follow the Chinese path. Production of wheat and rice will soon plummet, and irrigated lands will have to account for three-fifths of India's production of these grains and four-fifths of China's.

A great number of the most crowded cities in the world are situated in the hydrographic basins from which all available water is taken. Mexico City, Cairo, and Beijing cannot increase their consumption except by taking water from other basins or from reservoirs designed for irrigation. After China and India, a second group of countries will face significant deficits: Algeria, Egypt, Iran, Mexico, and Pakistan.

Agriculture will still have to face an enormous additional demand, with 70 million persons added to the world's population per year and with nearly 5 billion people desiring to consume more products of animal origin. Farmers will face a reduction in the amount of water available for irrigation, the warming of the planet, and an increase in the cost of fuels. Between 1950 and 1990, grain yields rose by 2.1 percent a year; since then they have fallen by 1.2 percent a year. Algeria, Egypt, and Mexico already import most of their grain. The food crisis observed in 2007, before it was provisionally extinguished by the subprime crisis, gives an idea of the challenges that will arise in this domain.

WHAT TO DO?

What should we do? What measures can be taken? Who should direct them? In many areas the diagnoses are already there; today the problem is how to go about the treatments. More than a decade ago, most countries joined in an international treaty, the Framework Convention of the UN on Climate Change, to "begin to consider what might be done to reduce global warming." A convention on biological diversity was also signed to meet the threat to the planet. A convention on the struggle against desertification was established to help threatened regions such as the Darfur region of Sudan. In 1994, the Cairo Conference on population and development fixed a plan of action designed to reduce infant mortality and to control demographic evolution. The plan calls for voluntary policies on education and health, including family planning and measures to prevent AIDS and other sexually transmitted diseases.

The so-called Millennium Declaration aims to reduce poverty and hunger and undereducation by half, and to improve "environmental sustainability"—before 2015. These objectives were reaffirmed during the Monterrey conference in 2002, during which a commitment was made to double public aid to development. However, despite these conventions, declarations of intent, and precise diagnoses of the problems and the means to resolve them, the world is spectacularly delayed in implementing these goals.

However, dealing with the problem of the ozone layer shows the speed with which public opinion may change on a subject that is reputedly sensitive. Originally, a scientific study showed the effect on the ozone layer of gases emitted by chlorofluorocarbons, which were used as a refrigerating gas and as a propelling agent in aerosols. The president of one of the market leaders, the DuPont Corporation, immediately responded that this was idiotic. But a little later, a NASA satellite aroused public opinion by showing shots of a growing hole above Antarctica. A convention was held the same year, and a protocol was rapidly signed in Montreal. DuPont acknowledged that there were indeed available alternatives and changed its position abruptly. In 1990, amendments were added to the Montreal protocol—under DuPont's influence, they are more restrictive that those initially called for.

Apart from this rather encouraging example, the gap between intentions and realization remains abysmal. The UN framework convention on climate change was signed in 1992 by President George H. W. Bush and ratified by the US Senate. The Kyoto Protocol adopted in 1997 for the period up to 2012 called for the rich countries to reduce their emissions of greenhouse gases by 8 percent. But the US Congress refused to ratify it, despite a signature by President Bill Clinton, and then the George W. Bush administration abandoned it. Barack Obama seemed more eager to act during its campaign, but not much has been achieved since.

A new industrial revolution

The debate often opposes the partisans of growth and the partisans of decrease. If growth is the mechanism that enables producing given goods at the least cost, or creating new goods that improve human life, then it appears to be more of a solution than a problem. But it still has to be directed along a path that is socially useful rather than futile. One of the misunderstandings about modern growth is as follows: It constantly improves industrial productivity, which reduces the number of hours necessary for the production of objects, and consequently their price. But the *volume* of objects doesn't decrease at all. Their price is lower, but their number continues to increase at a rapid pace. The always reduced price explains the takeoff of a "throwaway economy." Once a person owned a watch for life but now changes watches to match clothing. Cheap electronic gadgets received as premiums for subscribing to magazines aren't even opened.

But this "throwaway economy" is "on a collision course with the earth's geological limits," as Brown put it.[45] The cost of removing garbage from urban zones shoots up. New York was one of the first great cities to saturate its dumping sites; 12,000 tons of waste are produced each day. It takes 600 trailer trucks a day to remove the garbage from the city streets. In these conditions, in a growing number

———

of cases, the price of objects becomes lower than the environmental costs they incur. Oystein Dahle, the former vice president of Exxon for Norway, quoted by Lester Brown, summarized the problem this way: "Socialism collapsed because it did not allow the market to tell the economic truth. Capitalism may collapse because it doesn't allow the market to tell the ecological truth."[46]

A first axis of action to control this crisis is to tax polluters through a carbon tax, especially as regards the struggle against global warming. But such taxation requires an audit, and inspection that is sometimes more costly than simply imposing environmental norms on the sectors concerned (electricity, transport, construction, public works). Another priority is to suppress the subsidies that favor activities that are destructive of the environment, such as the overexploitation of aquifers, forest clear-cutting, and overfishing.

Investing in clean energies is the second direction. The main conclusion of the Stern Report is unequivocal. The earlier the problems are addressed, the less the cost. According to this report, a permanent annual investment of 1 percent of world GDP would suffice to fight global warming, on condition that this is begun immediately. The IPCC also estimates that the cost of generalizing the best technologies for capturing carbon might be modest.[47] But what seems today a reasonable effort may have an exorbitant cost if action is delayed.

But it will take much more than taxing, subsidizing, and investing. To succeed, the environmental revolution must produce changes that would amount to the equivalent of a new industrial revolution: a new way of conceiving of economic growth.

Consider, for example, the foreseen end of oil. The evolutions considered today to be natural, including urbanization and international exchanges, might be reversed from one day to the next under the pressures exerted when oil becomes rare and expensive. Despite the anticipated constraints, new aircraft are being delivered in the prospect of the aerial traffic of freight and passengers being extended indefinitely. The largest automobile corporation in the world, General Motors, was declared bankrupt in 2009, partly as a result of its having wagered on absurd "sport-utility vehicles."

The end of oil will challenge the functioning of an urban civilization based on the automobile, in which the suburbs play an essential role. The current model where people commute for an hour in their cars each day from their suburban homes to their places of work is slated for death. The whole economy of mobility must be rethought.

Collapse

Jared Diamond, in his book *Collapse: How Societies Choose to Fail or Succeed* (revised in 2011), analyzes the way in which many civilizations have succumbed to the ecological disasters that they had provoked. The Sumerians had developed the first cities and the first written language. But that civilization had a failing. The irrigation system made the level of aquifer layers rise, due to percolation. When this level reached a few centimeters from the surface, the water began to evaporate, producing soil that was very salty. In time, this salt accumulation affected the land's productivity. Today Sumer is a place where vegetation is rare, if not entirely absent.

The Mayan civilization had the same fate. Between its flourishing in 250 CE and its decline in 900 its agriculture was sophisticated and productive, but deforestation and soil erosion unleashed a food shortage that led to civil wars among the various cities, until they were eliminated from the map. Easter Island and the Vikings of Greenland are other examples of civilizations destroyed by their inability to meet an ecological challenge.

According to Diamond, these disasters are the results of four types of mistakes, four types of inabilities: to foresee the problems being created, to identify them correctly when they occur, to demonstrate the will to resolve them once they are identified, and to manage to do so once the desire is manifest.

We are already entering phase three. The problems were not anticipated, but by now they have been identified. What is lacking is, first, the collective will to face up to them and, second, the prospect that this will result in the means to resolve them. In all the areas cited, it will take a coordinated effort of scientific research and political decision making to agree on new international standards.

Here is one counterexample to pessimism. Six hundred years ago, Iceland realized that overexploitation of high pastures was leading to a loss of vegetation in a region where it was thin to begin with. Farmers then agreed to control the size of sheep flocks and to define quotas for preserving the potential of this land. The country survived the ecological risk. What makes this reference to Iceland still tragic is that the country did not survive the financial danger, the subprime one, in a crisis that offers a disturbing demonstration of our inability to anticipate systemic dangers.

14

The Financial Crash

The New Financial Capitalism

The production of wealth requires raw materials, labor, and capital. Globalization tends to give a geographic definition to these categories. Labor is in Asia, the raw materials are in Africa and the Middle East. And capital remains the privilege of rich countries. In the language of Marx, capital in economics has a double meaning: an advance on the funds necessary to buy machinery and rent manpower, and supervising the process of production. This idea remains insightful but the form in which it is exercised has changed. Capital has become an "immaterial" good. Intangibles—research and development, advertising, fashion, finance—now govern the world of production.

If poor countries play an increasing role in the production of material goods, rich countries have firmly kept their hands on immaterial production. R&D, to take a characteristic example, is the prerogative of rich countries, to the tune of 95 percent. Everything is done to investigate and find a cure for the illnesses that affect them (cancer, diabetes, Alzheimer's, and so on), but illnesses like malaria find no cure—for want of paying clients. Management by the rich countries of immaterial flows obeys a logic that in no way benefits the global good, alas. In the language of economists, private returns do not necessarily coincide with social returns.

The subprime crisis is an outstanding instance, showing the inability of the financial industry—the supreme form of immaterial flows—to appreciate the risks that it was making the planet run. Diamond's four phases of collapse unfolded: incapacity to foresee the crisis, to identify it when the first signs appeared, to agree on what should then be done, and to execute the actions to tackle the crisis. Let us take up this dreadful sequence.

The crisis of Keynesianism

The unbridled period that opened in the 1980s dismantled the old regulated and cooperative world that had been forged after World War II. In economic matters, this had been underpinned by a triangle associated with the names Ford, Beveridge, and Keynes. First, Fordism was challenged by the dismantling of firms that was orchestrated in the 1980s. The social benefits underlying the solidarity promoted by William Beveridge in Britain in the 1940s (see chapter 9) ran up against a slowing of growth at the end of the postwar boom. Finally, the Keynesian argument was itself called into question; the idea that macroeconomic regulation was necessary for the good functioning of capitalism became an archaic idea—before the subprime crisis abruptly restored it to its place of honor.

The challenge to Keynesianism dates from the 1970s, and the break was apparent during the oil price shock. The OPEC countries quadrupled the price of petroleum in 1973 and doubled it again in 1978. This spectacular rise would entrain economies down the road to a new evil, hard to define in the beginning. "Stagflation" was an unprecedented mixture of inflation and recession; this phenomenon was only belatedly understood by economists and politicians. Trained in Keynesian arguments since the end of the war, they had learned to analyze economic cycles as manifestations of imbalances in demand. When demand is weak, there is unemployment but inflation tends to decrease. When demand is strong, it is the opposite: Unemployment decreases but inflation rises. This inverse relation would be described by the Phillips Curve (named after A. William Phillips, the economist who demonstrated it in 1956).

But stagflation upset this relation. In effect, there was not one or the other of the two evils (inflation or unemployment), but both at once. Understanding this apparent paradox took some time. It was not that the demand had become insufficient. Rather, the supply had abruptly ceased being profitable—first as a result of the upward spiral in oil prices, more durably because of exhaustion of the rise in productivity. Focusing on the demand, even when the supply was weak, governments accelerated the rise in prices without reducing unemployment. All governments—in France, both Valéry Giscard d'Estaing's on the right and François Mitterrand's on the left—would fail when they tried to make a boosting of consumption the instrument of the struggle against unemployment.

This failure would open the way to a formidable challenge. Politicians and economists in the 1980s would come up with a counterview to Keynes, relying on Milton Friedman, the grand master of Chicago, and his disciples, who were called neo-monetarists. They advocated the withdrawal of the state from economic affairs and denounced the welfare state as the culprit in the loss of business competitiveness. The market was posited as infallible, and thus unemployment was "natural." In Friedman's eyes, the economic policies of Keynesian inspiration were aggravating the problem they were trying to fight. By wanting to reach full employment at all costs, Keynesian policies were triggering an acceleration of inflation, which then became very costly to control.

The determining event of this sequence was the monetary policy conducted by Paul Volcker, the new chairman of the Federal Reserve at the start of the 1980s. Wanting to break inflation, he abruptly reduced the money supply, provoking an increase in interest rates. From 1982 to 1984, as a result of Volcker's shock therapy, inflation fell abruptly in the United States. At the cost of a considerable recession, the "credibility" of American monetary policy was finally restored, and confidence in the currency returned.[48] Inversely, confidence in Keynesian precepts disappeared. This was the climate in which the neo-classical revolution of the 1980s occurred.

The new spirit of capitalism

The industrial capitalism issuing from the great Fordist tradition had prospered in the shadow of the crisis of the 1930s and in that of the Cold War. After 1929 the Stock Exchange had been discredited, morally and economically, being held responsible for the crisis and the war. Company directors now acted on the idea they held of the good of the firm, royally ignoring the stockholders. It was the golden age of what might be called managerial capitalism. The Cold

War also played a role, as the philosopher Peter Sloterdijk wryly remarked; it was a period when European wage earners could easily obtain satisfaction for their demands: "It sufficed for them to consider the realities of the Second World [the Soviet bloc] to make it clear to the employers that here, too, social peace had its price."[49]

After the 1980s the shareholders decided to take the upper hand. They engaged in an overhaul of the organization of labor that prevailed after the war—calling into question career plans, social benefits, unions. Bonuses were substituted for career plans; in short order, managers (until then salaried like everyone else) were brought to the forefront, seeing their salaries indexed to stock prices, to which they would submit since they were now responsible for them. It was the death of one type of capitalism and the birth of another.

The norm that the new "stockholder society" would dictate consisted of reducing the activity of a firm to the single area corresponding to the firm's "core competitive advantage." All the rest was left to the market. The outsourcing of tasks became the rule. In a business of the 1950s and the 1960s, cafeteria service, landscaping, cleaning, and accounting were all performed by employees of the company. With outsourcing, none of these services was now provided internally, and bidders for them were put into competition. We are tending toward corporations that dream of having no employees at all, a process that is accelerated by the revolution in information and communication technologies. With globalization enlarging competition and offering cheaper labor, this movement is going to reach its culmination. Domestic outsourcing gives way to sending work abroad when possible. But, as the chronology shows, the internal reorganization of capitalism preceded globalization.

The financial markets

This revolution would also upset the financial system itself. A new set of financial intermediaries—free of the regulations set up after the 1929 crisis—was developing. This new system is sometimes called the "shadow banking system." Having started from almost nothing in the 1980s, in the United States on the eve of the subprime crisis, it was worth as much as the traditional banking system: $10 trillion. The shadow banking system consists of investors' banks or hedge funds, private equity funds (which buy unquoted companies on credit), and insurance companies.[50] To maximize their profits from the opportunities created by this new financial market, banks created unprecedented special investment vehicles (SIVs) that were off the balance sheet. By locating their new activities in these *ad hoc* vehicles, the banks, too, freed themselves from prudential regulations. They could profit to the maximum from the "leveraging" effect (the possibility of financing on credit operations with high returns) without mobilizing their own funds.

The financial market accomplished in its own way Wall Street's new dream: fabricating companies "without factories and without workers." The traditional banks had to continue to accept, through their branches, deposits from individuals. They had to conduct investigations of their customers for any demand for a loan, to follow them over time until maturity, and to carry the risk of default. But modern finance was going to free itself from these painful activities. Sitting in front of their computer screens, traders and others would finance only via the market, ignoring the constraint of collecting deposits from individuals. Instead of granting credit, traders would "securitize" it—meaning put it on the market after having "recomposed" it with loans given by others. This new system would thus externalize all the classic functions performed by the commercial bank—collecting deposits and distributing loans—and prosper on a single expertise: financial engineering. Everything was now in place for the greatest failure in financial history.

There was one innovation that could indeed be called inspired. To make real-estate loans more attractive, Wall Street's "rocket scientists" joined together and then cut into slices the portfolios of mortgage lenders. The better slices were paid off first, the second later, and so on, with the last slice undergoing the risk of possible default. Thus they manufactured a varied palette of assets that was interesting to a vast array of investors: pension funds for the better slices, hedge funds for risky assets, and so on. The banks kept (off the books) the assets no one wanted. "Subprime," an invention finalized in 1983 by a subsidiary of General Electric, was originally designed for common borrowers. Despite a crisis in 1994, this practice took off in the 2000s, widening the range of households able to benefit from a loan. The most disadvantaged strata of the working class— those whose risk was least good, the "subprimes"—finally had access to credit. Wall Street was coming to the rescue of Harlem. But the fairy tale turned out badly.

The subprime crisis was triggered by several delayed bombshells. First of all, upstream of the crisis, one factor was rapidly revealed. The quality of the loans had deteriorated badly, even if one takes into account the new clientele to which it was addressed. The solvency of clients was systematically overestimated by the intermediaries charged with distributing loans. The cause of this degradation was evident. With the securitization of loans, the person at the initial source of the credit had immediately resold it to the financial markets. The incentive had changed completely. What counted was the turnover, not keeping an eye on the quality of the clients. Granting credit while knowing that it will be immediately passed on is not the same thing as making a loan that one will have to recover oneself. Apart from the negligence, it was established that fraud had been committed. Some lenders had artificially inflated the solvency of their clients in order to increase their turnover figures.

Distrust concerning the quality of securities also can be attributed to the methods used to evaluate risk. With the help of rating agencies, investors fabricated instruments that were supposedly risk-free. To do so they used sophisticated mathematical models that predicted the probability of default on any type of credit, so the least risky part could be extracted. These models perform well in normal times, but according to *The Economist* they led Goldman Sachs to close a fund whose probability of default had been estimated at one in 10 to the power of 138.[51]

The financial market thus tried to circulate "false financial currency"—securities whose quality hadn't been verified. This offhand behavior, this blindness to risk, was the essential factor in the crash.

GREED

In his classic book *The Protestant Ethic and the Rise of Capitalism*, published in 1904, Max Weber explained that capitalism is not characterized by greed or a desire for money. If it were, it would have developed in the Middle East among Phoenician merchants, or in Venice among spice traders. But instead it appeared in England, then developed in the United States and in Northern Europe. Although Weber recognized that greed is one of the basic springs of human activity, he maintained that capitalism rationalized this appetite, constructing relations of trust and contract, and reequilibrating it all with rules, laws, and an "ethic" of responsibility.

The financial revolution shows how fragile this Weberian view of capitalism is. One of the striking traits of the new spirit of capitalism that emerged in the 1980s is the extravagant rise in inequality. The data of Thomas Piketty and Emmanuel Saez[52] show that in the United States the top 1 percent of the rich have regained the position they had at the turn of the twentieth century, in the golden age of capitalism; they now earn more than 20 percent of the national income, as opposed to only 7 percent after the war. This is truly the reign of "crazy money."

According to the *Financial Times*, in the three years that preceded the crisis the CEOs of the major financial firms accumulated nearly $100 billion in income. The losses they left to the community as a whole amounted to $4 trillion. This effect of "inverse" leverage illustrates the mechanism that was at work.

From the moment when traders and financiers entirely finance themselves on credit to increase their operations, a perverse incentive is created. If credit generates profits, traders and financiers pay off their debt and share the profits with the investor who financed them. If the investment is "bad credit" (insolvent), the losses fall entirely upon the lender. But when an investor doesn't bring his own capital, the game becomes "tails I win, heads you lose." For the financiers who earned $100 billion for $4 trillion in losses, the bottom line was always positive. Whatever was done afterward, this loss could never be privatized by making those who were guilty pay back the billions they had caused society to lose.

The economist and columnist Paul Krugman characterized the attitude of these financial leaders as "Panglossian." Voltaire's hero Pangloss believes he sees "the best of all possible worlds" everywhere.[53] The trader does the same; he sees only the good side of things, he ignores the risk, not myopically, but rationally, because the principle of remuneration is asymmetric. If he wins, he wins everything; if he loses, he may lose his job, perhaps even his career, but his loss will never be proportional to what he makes others suffer.

It is not only actors in the financial market who are entrained in this spiral. Households are also enticed to adopt risky behavior. In the United States a very lax arrangement allows them in effect to increase their debt as the value of their real estate increases. Each hike in property prices is an opportunity for them to reschedule their debt, to the maximum of the capital gain—and to spend more.

An astonishing statistic will give an indication of the eagerness of American households to consume. Even though income inequalities did not cease growing in the 1990s and the 2000s, we observe no visible hike in inequalities of consumption. Credit has entirely replaced income as the motor of growth. Thus the subprime crisis is the expression of the pathological behavior of a society that has decided to forget the reality principle and to live in the virtual world of virtual capital gains.

Everything goes fine as long as property prices continue rising. But everything tips over when prices begin to fall. Households whose recourse to debts is higher than the value of their purchased goods simply stop reimbursing the debt, unless they are able to obtain new credit allowing them to refinance it. Like financial establishments betting on risk, American households have ignored the risk of the cycle turning around. And when property prices finally began to fall, the house of cards fabricated by the Panglosses of finance could only collapse.

THE COLLAPSE

When the subprime crisis broke out, during the summer of 2007, Chairman Ben Bernanke of the Federal Reserve was without doubt the person the best qualified to hold that post. Bernanke had written academic books that had helped demonstrate decisively the responsibility of American monetary authorities for the crisis of the 1930s. From the beginning of the crisis, he did not hesitate to inject considerable liquidity into the economy. He didn't balk at saving the investment bank Bear Stearns, then the mortgage lenders Freddie Mac and Fannie Mae.

Bernanke inherited an explosive situation that been handed to him by his predecessor, Alan Greenspan. Believing that the risk of inflation had been eradicated, Greenspan had conducted a policy of easy money throughout his term (August 1987–January 2006), creating in turn the Internet bubble and the real-estate bubble. It was under his leadership that the financial market, living on credit, had prospered before it imploded with the subprime crisis.

Even Bernanke, though, ended up committing the error he had criticized in his writings. By allowing Lehman Brothers to fail on Monday September 15, 2008, he provoked the shock waves that triggered the explosion. All treasurers of businesses understood that the refinancing of their credit, more or less insured in the course of the past year, was no longer guaranteed. Firms began to liquidate their inventories, to reduce their investments. Household morality was broken.

Recall that in Milton Friedman's interpretation of the 1930s crisis it was bank failures that had been the real cause. Now everything was being done to save the threatened banks. Under the Paulson

Plan, $700 billion was quickly mobilized to avoid new catastrophes, not without sharpening the popular sentiment that the bankers were being compensated for their past vices—"Wall Street bailed out by Main Street." Everything unfolded as if the failure of a single bank had produced effects comparable to the real failure of most American banks in the 1930s. The whole financial market came tumbling down from the fall of the first domino.

But the Keynesian interpretation has not been surpassed in explaining the recent crisis. In 2008 as in 1929, the purchasing of "durable goods" was in the front line. In 2008 as in 1930, the automobile industry was hit in the midst of a boom. General Motors found itself failing, and Toyota announced losses for the first time in its history. The other great sector affected, as in 1930, was housing, the sector in which the crisis began. As those inspired by Keynes explain, the decrease in household and business spending unleashed a multiplier mechanism that amplified the crisis. And as in 1930, the collapse of world trade brutally retroacted on national conjectures.

Lessons of the crisis

The debate between Keynes and Friedman cannot be reduced to the question of whether the banks should be saved or whether consumption should be stimulated. In the heat of the crisis, it was clear that both had to be done at the same time. The real debate is about the nature of market economies. Friedman was convinced that a market economy can stabilize itself all alone, provided that one leaves it alone, pushing the paradox by adding that in fact government actions are a factor of instability.

Keynes thought exactly the opposite. One of his wisest commentators, Axel Leijonhuvfud, summed up this opposition on the basis of a metaphor called the "corridor." The forces pulling an economy toward an equilibrium of full employment can function in the desired direction, but only inside a corridor of confidence. When growth slows, one can wait, under certain conditions, for households to draw on their savings to maintain their consumption, for businesses to profit from the fall in interest rates to invest, and so on. But past a certain threshold of crisis, as when a car is skidding off the road, the economy no longer comes back to its "natural" state. It careens, and the forces driving it aggravate the crisis. Faced with a slowdown, households save instead of spending, and businesses stop their investments instead of increasing them. Fear sets in, and the most vulnerable financial establishments go bankrupt. The laws of the economy become pathological.

The subprime crisis was a reminder for those who wanted to forget the power of Keynesian reasoning. Without the determined intervention of the authorities, who nevertheless had passively watched Lehman go under, this crisis probably would have followed, step by step, that of 1929. Less than 25 years after the financial revolution that thought it could "forget '29," the crisis had come back—and in the same guise. A world left to the sole forces of "every man for himself" is a mirage that must have been forgotten; 25 years after the financial revolution, capitalism must now tend its wounds and rethink its criteria. The lesson of Keynes was heard again.

The lessons one might draw from the subprime crisis go beyond this rediscovery of the state's role. The speed with which the collapse was propagated to the world economy testifies to the extraordinary difficulty of *ex ante* conceiving of systemic risks, and of reabsorbing them, *ex post facto*, when they become manifest.

Andrew Haldane, who is responsible for financial risks at the Bank of England, has proposed an interesting parallel between the world of the financial market and that of the electricity grid.[54] Interconnection allows partial imbalances between supply and demand to be resolved. When one network suffers excess demand, it can count on the others to supply power. Interconnection functions as a shock absorber. But past a critical threshold, the opposite is produced. A local malfunction, even a minor one, can put everything in danger, plunging even regions distant from the breakdown into the dark.

Haldane also offers, in the same paper, an illuminating comparison between the financial crisis and pandemics. One of the lessons of studies in biology and epidemiology is that a crisis may become fatal when the complexity of a system is accompanied by a loss of diversity. A statistical study has shown that 40 percent of fish species have disappeared, but the percentage reaches 60 in zones where resources are homogeneous and falls to 10 in regions with strong species diversity. Similarly, the accumulation of defects is much more frequent in incestuous families (like the Hapsburg dynasty, which was plunged into sterility). By contact with other species, by diversifying its genetic legacy, each can immunize itself against the sicknesses that threaten it. Diversity is a reducer of risk.

In the case of the financial market, uniform behavior was the rule. All the actors wanted to do the same thing. Cooperative credit unions wanted to become banks; the commercial banks wanted to become investment banks; investment banks wanted to become venture capital and hedge funds. From the outside, no one could even judge the pertinence of the strategies being adopted. And so all of them succumbed, at the same time, to the same illness.

This is where we are. World capitalism now dominates like a civilization that substitutes itself for all others, without external oversight to judge its pertinence. Economic and cultural interconnection has become the rule, which subjects everybody to the risk of global dysfunction.

15

The Weightless Economy

The New Economy

Among the aberrant traits of contemporary capitalism that the sub-prime crisis threw into relief were the salaries of company directors who are paid as much as rock stars and the reckless risks they take as a result of their Panglossian outlook. There was now no doubt in the eyes of most commentators that the "empire of greed" should be policed. If it were still just a matter of financial problems strictly speaking, the solution would be simple: impose sufficiently strict and prudent norms on all the actors in finance, within and outside their balance sheets. But the breadth of the issues was much vaster, and another transformation was at work, with weighty corollaries. The subprime crisis was only an early symptom of a new phenomenon: the emergence of an economy that is de-materialized and weightless, or what might be called the entry into the cyber-world of information and communication technologies.

The term "the new economy" refers to a radical modification of the usual paradigm of the economy as it was analyzed by Adam Smith and Karl Marx. (See chapter 5.) Smith explained that if it takes twice as long to hunt a buck as to hunt a beaver, the former will necessarily cost, on average, twice as much as the latter. The "new economy" is characterized by a cost structure that is atypical of this normal scheme. A piece of software is expensive to conceive but not to manufacture. Once the Windows software was conceived, it could just as well be sold to one village as to the whole world, since its manufacturing cost would be only marginally modified. The same reasoning applies to the media—for example, a movie costs a lot to produce, but not to (re-)run. More generally, information content (whether it takes the form of a digital code, a symbol, or a molecule) costs much more to conceive than the physical form in which it is harbored.

In this new economy, it is the first unit of the manufactured good that is onerous to make; the cost of the second (and all those following) is low, if not nil (as it is in certain limit cases). In the language of Adam Smith, we would have to say that the time spent killing the first beaver or the first buck—meaning the time spent finding where they have gone to ground—would explain all the costs. And in the language of Karl Marx, we would have to say that the source of surplus value lies not in the work devoted to producing the object, but in what happens when it is conceived. The person who manufactures the object is no longer a source of (substantial) profit. He is a cost, perhaps to be outsourced.

A typical example is that of drugs. The most difficult thing is to discover the molecule. The cost of manufacturing the drug itself, as measured by the price of generic medicines, is much lower than the amortization of the R&D expenditures that are factored into charges for those drugs under license.

This paradigm also involves industrial firms. In its advertising campaign, Renault, formerly a symbol of industrial society, now wants to present itself as a "conceiver" of automobiles. And in fact this French company now tends to manufacture a smaller and smaller portion of the cars that bear its brand name. In the 1950s, Renault manufactured 80 percent of the car that was delivered to the dealer. Today it makes only 20 percent. The "technopolis" at Guyancourt is Renault's largest "industrial" site, but its purpose is to fabricate the first unit. If we are to believe an anecdote that typifies this evolution, the Head of Purchasing at Volkswagen in Brazil congratulates himself that his firm has managed to outsource most of the manufacturing, leaving it up to the German firm to do what it knows how to do best: put the brand insignia on the front of the car. In the time of globalization, companies are trying to recenter themselves on activities of planetary scope, those that touch the greatest number of customers. Immaterial activities, in which the cost lies in making the first unit or promoting the brand name, are much more profitable than the actual manufacturing of goods that result from it.[55]

"Post-industrial" society unites two opposite terms: the one that corresponds to the conception of (immaterial) goods and the one that relates to their prescription (commercialization). The chemical formula contained in a drug is immaterial. The doctor prescribing the correct drug lies in the domain described by Fourastié through the example of the barber, a job of proximity that cannot be robotized or performed at a distance. The barber, the doctor, and the repairman escape globalization, since they all work face to face with their clients. The producer of immaterial goods, inversely, is immediately plunged into a great sea of globalization. Any patented molecule in principle has a vocation to cure all human bodies, as far away as they may be from the laboratory that discovered it.

Face to face remains within the habitual order of Smith's or Marx's economy. Its actors are paid competitively for the time they spend with their clients. The working hour remains the pertinent accounting unit to evaluate their payment. Immaterial production is quite different. A movie actor is not paid in proportion to the time spent in making a film. He is paid as a function of his celebrity, in the market where his appearance alone (whether it lasts two minutes or two hours) enables him to command a fee.

From an economic point of view, immaterial production thrives under the reign of increasing returns. The larger the share of a market a producer possesses, the easier it is for him to amortize the cost of conception of a new good, and the more money he can earn. The new economy appears as the end result of a process that has made the economy move from the age of decreasing returns (agricultural production) to the age of constant returns (industrial production), and finally to the age of increasing returns (immaterial production). It should be noted that these three dimensions are always present, simultaneously, in each of the three stages that one might associate with rural, industrial, and post-industrial societies. Agriculture and industry were always intimately dependent on technological innovations to pursue their courses. What is new in the current period relates to the fact that technological advances tend to acquire an autonomous force, dictating to other sectors a rhythm that is becoming incumbent on us all.

The new economy is sometimes associated with the ideas of better dissemination of information, lower barriers to entry, and stronger competitive pressure on the actors in the economy. However, its own operators tend to become global monopolies. There is a curious analogy between property income from rural production and front-line technologies. Owing to the law of increasing returns, the dominant company outdistances the others and tends to acquire an impregnable position. Microsoft, Apple, and Google dominate the market to the point that they are now outside the range of their competitors, especially European ones, thanks to a logic that pushes toward concentration. We now understand why the production of immaterial goods has become the comparative advantage of rich countries.

Europe lagging behind

Joseph Needham's question (Why didn't China produce a Newton and a Galileo?) has now become this question: Why have the great universities and the best research centers become the privilege of rich countries, and singularly the richest of them all, the United States?

For a European to be aware of American supremacy, it suffices to open his computer in the morning when he arrives at his desk and to turn on the television when getting home in the evening. From the Windows software to TV series such as *24* and *Desperate Housewives*, immaterial globalization shows that it speaks English. The globalization of the twenty-first century is that of technologies coming from Silicon Valley, governance standards coming from Wall Street, and films made in Hollywood.

———

Faced with this preeminence, Europe is indisputably in difficulty. It keeps its rank in the pharmaceutical industry, but it is behind in all other recent developments: computing, nanotechnology, biotechnology. Yet it is a rich continent, possessing a huge domestic market and numerous "humanoids" in Robert Solow's sense. So why this lag?

Europe's first problem relates to the institutions dedicated to teaching and research. The production of knowledge requires (in the era of globalization) strong universities that protect researchers from the short-term thinking of industrialists, but without letting them ignore economic demands. In the course of the "long Middle Ages" that preceded the Industrial Revolution, Europe combined rivalry among its nations and a unity of thought borne by the Latin of a shared culture. Today, exactly the opposite is at work. Nation-states want to cooperate, but European research remains an assortment of national research programs that as a whole are worth less than the sum of the parts. Even the procedures Brussels uses for allocating European Community funds remain very attentive to respecting the balance among nations, and Europe has not managed to produce European centers comparable to those that sprang up around the best American universities.

The other aspect of American supremacy relates to the role played by the Department of Defense. It is a direct architect of the race for innovation, financing both very applied projects and very weird ones. The Department of Defense makes R&D the stake in a war that is itself tending to become virtual and immaterial, constantly pushing American technologies to outstrip those elsewhere. Technology establishes the United States' role as a global military power—something Europe no longer aspires to be.

The historian and foreign policy commentator Robert Kagan, who is close to neo-conservative circles, depicts the contrast between Europe and the United States as a new form of conflict between Mars and Venus. He explains that the Americans are on the side of Mars (war), and Europeans on the side of Venus (love). This image exasperates many Europeans, since they would like to establish a European military power capable of participating in the conduct of world affairs on the same level as America.

This comparison is faithful enough to the respective roles of the two continents, but it doesn't have the condescending meaning that is attributed to it. Europeans know—even if they find it hard to admit—exactly where the path that they once opened can lead. Europe is the one region of the world that has gone to the end of a historical path on which the rest of the planet is now embarked. Americans ignore—or want to forget—the tragic dimension of Western history. They left Europe in the eighteenth century, taking with them that century's philosophy, resolutely optimistic about the capacity of people to organize rationally a society freed from its superstitions.

The United States is scarcely sensitive to the complaints of the Romantic writers of the nineteenth century; it remains resolutely convinced that the new is worth more than the old, almost by definition. Americans find it hard to give language to the difficulty of other countries that are mourning a lost world. Samuel Huntington writes: "Somewhere in the Middle East, a half dozen young men would be well dressed in jeans, drinking Coke, listening to rap, and between their bows to Mecca, putting together a bomb to blow up an American airliner."[56] Here he is conveying the ambiguity of the sentiment that the rest of the world feels for America and the difficulty America has understanding that.

In the Cyber-World

American success is just as patent in the cultural realm as in the technological or financial realms, owing in part to the same laws. Thanks to its domestic market, America possesses a formidable field of internal selection for the titles that will be most attractive. American publishers and producers, after having sorted these out, may then distribute bestsellers and blockbusters to international markets.

The culture industries (films, television, music, books, etc.) provide an excellent key to understanding the mechanisms at work in the cyber-world of information and communication technologies. The culture industry functions on the "star system" principle, analyzed by Françoise Benhamou.[57] In a world that people believe is open to diversity, in fact a very small number of works—whether films, songs, books, or exhibitions—carry all the investment bets. People all want to see, hear, or read the same thing. There are several reasons for that.

When information becomes too abundant, mimetic behavior remains the best way to select that which is pertinent. (If the film is a hit, it is because it is good.) Then the quest for social connections means that one wants to see the same films or TV programs as other people do, in order to be able to talk about them together the next day. Finally, for these very reasons, promotional techniques push investors to bet everything on the product that is a sure hit.

This star system has a direct influence on the status and the remuneration of the artist. An example borrowed from another world will help us understand its import. Why, Steve Levitt and Stephen Dubner asked in their 2005 book *Freakonomics*, do drug traffickers live with their mothers? The answer was that they don't have the means to do otherwise. While the leader of a gang earns a fortune, his subordinates live miserably. So why do they remain drug dealers? Because they dream of becoming the leader. This is also the model of remuneration in the creative industries today. Artists live miserably, except for the stars. And everybody accepts this, because every artist aspires to become a star. In the star system, the winner takes all. This explains why the bosses, living in the world of top brands and fame, find it "fair" that their salaries are fixed by the same rules, forgetting John Pierpont Morgan's remark that a company whose president earns more than twenty times the salary of one of his employees cannot function well. But these days the remuneration of a CEO is worth 200 times the income of one of his employees.

In the cultural realm, the organization of the world arranges a sharing of tasks between Hollywood and the national industries that has been well described by the American economist Tyler Cowen.[58] Hollywood deals with "universal" subjects (money, sex, violence) for a worldwide audience. National producers complement this offer by producing at lower cost the great themes of their country's realities. In France we appreciate Sophie Marceau because we knew her when she was little and she is part of our national film culture, but we revere Al Pacino and Robert De Niro, who are like Olympian gods, both far from ordinary men and near to them.[59] Stars of intermediate rank—European ones, for example—have no relevance. The world of the culture industries lives in a dual mode, the infinitely near and the infinitely far. Cultural globalization can be summarized as a duel between national producers and American producers. The threat that hovers over national production is less to be feared than the disadvantages of openness "to the world," which essentially amounts to importing from the United States.

Book publishing, not the highest-tech sector, is a good example of the process at work. In France, 40 percent of the novels that are published are translations, three-fourths of them from English.[60] The same phenomenon is found in music and in television. The "prime-time" TV shows in France are principally French, but the foreign ones are almost exclusively American.[61]

The death of Malthus

It is on the terrain of globalization of images that the oldest economic law in the world, Malthus' Law, is reaching its terminus. The demographic transition that puts an end to the hold of birth rates over human destiny seems to be directly linked to the dissemination by TV of the "American" model of the liberated woman. UN experts predict that by 2050 most women the world over will, as in the West, be bearing an average of 1.85 children. According to the same experts, this phenomenon seems to be explained more by the diffusion of cultural behavior than by any "cost/benefit" theory. The argument of economists that the demographic transition results from new material conditions, with women who want to work having fewer children, doesn't seem to be determining in actual fact. For example, it can be observed in cities as in the countryside, and among both working and non-working women. Everywhere, demographic behavior is in advance of material reality, thanks to the world of images.[62]

In fact, the number of television sets seems to be a more direct determinant of the fall in demographics than income level, or even education level. The demographic transition occurs more quickly in Brazil, a great consumer of *telenovelas*, than in Mexico, where family planning has been more important. In Asia, young women emulate young Japanese women, who emulate American women.[63] Demographic evolution on its own is the essential part of the overall transition of the rural Malthusian world into the modern urban world. It is astonishing and remarkable how much this transformation owes to the intrusion of images and telecommunications into the developing countries.

Yet the virtual world is not always a good guide. The cyberworld is a school of schizophrenia between the dream life and real life, between virtual violence and actual violence. In comparison with a video game, the laws of ordinary life seem burdensome to an adolescent. Crossing a street becomes boring when you can no longer defy the laws of gravity.[64] Yet youth everywhere must be prepared to learn the new limits of the planet. The Roman Empire died from being enclosed in a shell of "cognitive indifference" to the world of production. Today, the gamble is to maintain the contact between the cyber-world and the actual world and its real limits. For many young people who applaud Al Gore's film on global warming or are active in non-governmental organizations while tapping on their keyboards, this link between worlds seems obvious. For them, a new mental construction is at work that ties together the virtual world and the ecosystem. It is on the strength of this reflection that the future of the twenty-first century will depend.

Conclusion

Since the dawn of time, humanity has walked a tightrope between two opposing forces. The number of human beings never ceases to grow, regularly running up against the scarceness of land to feed them. But by their very number, people multiply the number of discoveries, pushing back the frontiers of knowledge, and continue their course, augmenting the density and complexity of social life. Sometimes civilizations die, falling on the wrong side of this equation. Powerless to understand what is happening to them, they are consumed, either slowly (as the Roman Empire was) or suddenly (as the Mayans were). Forgetting about these lost civilizations sometimes allows us to think that humankind always comes through, but only by omitting the cases in which it didn't manage to do so.

But once in history, an unprecedented acceleration of the production of knowledge enabled a portion of humankind to be enriched in the long term. The possibility of perpetual growth was born in Europe somewhere between the twelfth and eighteenth centuries, entraining a self-catalytic process in which wealth seemed to engender itself. This process is today being disseminated to the whole planet, provoking what might be called a Westernization of the world.

At first sight, material prosperity is an unhoped-for gift. It makes hunger disappear, lengthens life expectancy, and reduces the working time necessary to produce useful goods. But from the standpoint of moral sentiments it is an ambivalent gift. It pacifies society, but only for a while, until society revises its requirements upward. The fertility of Prometheus is constantly neutralized by the voracity of his sister-in-law Pandora. The textbook image of a society made peaceful thanks to the virtues of "gentle commerce" doesn't stand up to examination. Economic development in no way instigates an eradication of violence. From the wars of religion in the sixteenth century to the world wars of the twentieth, violence has been primarily constrained in response to its own excesses.

Today it is the turn of the emerging countries to start off along the escarpments that lead to the industrial world and to urban civilization. To do so, they must condense into a few decades the transformations that European countries experienced over several centuries. The explosion of violence that was manifested after the fall of the Berlin Wall shows the concentrations of resentment and hatred that remain to be vented. There is nothing "cultural" (in Huntington's sense) about this explosion. Well before the mullahs, the composer Richard Wagner was already denouncing "Paris, Europe, and the West" as a "corrupt, commercial, and frivolous world—which is not yet found in our provincial Germany, so comfortable with its outmoded aspect." Contemplating the current world, Europe has a hard time recognizing itself in the mirror held up to it.

But recent history is not just a repetition. It opens a new frontier: the cyber-world that has been fabricated by new technologies.
Wars themselves are becoming virtual. The "Third World War"—
the Cold War—was won by the United States on the terrain of the
new post-industrial world. The missile-defense program initiated by
President Ronald Reagan demonstrated symbolically to the USSR
that it had lost the technological war with the US. Knowing that it
wasn't capable of answering this new challenge, the USSR collapsed
without a fight.

The attack of September 11, 2001 also belongs to this third
type of violence, analyzed by Robert Muchembled, which aims at
the imaginary.[1] By symbolically targeting Wall Street and the Penta-
gon in an event witnessed by millions of viewers, al-Qaeda declared
war on America on the terrain that now seems to be the only one
that counts: the virtual world. The attack in 2001 was itself organized
in the manner of a Hollywood film. The first plane that hit one of
the two towers guaranteed that the second hit would be seen all over
the world. Al-Qaeda's terrorism is ferociously postmodern; it is in
the image of the virtual world created by the Internet. The very
term "terrorist network" illustrates this new dimension of globalization, which is able to connect all points of the globe. Al-Qaeda
perfectly incarnates this new dimension. All the young men of Muslim origin, whether living in Gujarat, on the border between India
and Pakistan, or in French suburbs, discovered they belonged to a
virtual community, whose thinking pulled them into the situation of
exploited minorities that they had suffered in their own countries.

In the new language, the questions posed in cyberspace are
always the same: What lives among people, what is part of oneself,
what is part of us? But the new world of planetary communication

redesigns the reference groups to which people compare themselves. To be happy no longer means just earning more than one's brother-in-law; now the comparison is with other cyber-communities, some distant in space but close in the virtual world. Young people who dramatize themselves on Facebook are learning this new space in their own way. Dreaming of being stars, they fabricate their new reference groups cybernetically.

September 11 proves that the violence of the cyber-world is no less murderous than the other kinds, but that is not the most serious issue. The central question posed by the new age of global communication is whether it will be capable of addressing the major issues of the twenty-first century: how to manage the anticipated ecological crisis and how to transform the norms of Western consumption in such a way as to make them compatible with their becoming generalized to the rest of the world.

At a time when it is tempting to wander about in the cyber-world, humankind should accomplish a cognitive task as immense as that realized during the Neolithic revolution or the Industrial Revolution: to learn to live within the limits of a solitary planet. For the first time in its history, humankind can no longer be allowed to correct its mistakes after the fact. It must mentally take the opposite path to the one that Europe has followed since the seventeenth century, and shift from the idea of an infinite world to a closed universe. This effort is not impossible or even improbable; more simply, it is not certain.[2] This very uncertainty has become the oppressive factor in human history, at a moment when, for the first time, humankind is betting its fate on the advent of a single world civilization.

Notes

Notes to Part I

1. Jacques Cauvin, *The Birth of the Gods and the Origins of Agriculture*, tr. T. Watkins (Cambridge University Press, 2000).

2. Ibid., p. 72.

3. Joel Mokyr, *The Lever of Riches: Technological Creativity and Economic Progress* (Oxford University Press, 1990).

4. Aldo Schiavone, *The End of the Past: Ancient Rome and the Modern West*, tr. M. Schneider (Harvard University Press, 2000), pp. 153, 147.

5. Ibid., p. 162.

6. Ibid., pp. 196–197.

7. Henri Mendras, *The Vanishing Peasant*, tr. J. Lerner (MIT Press, 1971), p. 24.

8. See Douglas North and Robert Thomas, *The Rise of the Western World: A New Economic History* (Cambridge University Press, 1973).

9. Jacques Le Goff, *Un autre Moyen Age* (Gallimard Quarto, 1996).

10. Ronald Findlay and Kevin O'Rourke, *Power and Plenty: Trade, War and the World Economy* (Princeton University Press, 2007).

11. Roger Pol Droit, *L'Occident expliqué a tout le monde* (Éditions du Seuil, 2008).

12. Schiavone, *The End of the Past*, pp. 144–145.

13. Alexandre Koyré, *From the Closed World to the Infinite Universe* (Johns Hopkins University Press, 1957), p. 205.

14. Ibid, pp. vii–viii.

15. Eric Jones, *The European Miracle* (Cambridge University Press, 1981).

16. Even if in Europe a good number of seigneurial privileges would remain until the French Revolution.

17. Robert Muchembled, *Une histoire de violence* (Fayard, 2008).

18. Norbert Elias, *The Civilizing Process: The History of Manners*, tr. E. Jephcott (Urizen, 1978). Elias imputes to the codes of civility that took effect in the monarch's court the rise in a civilization of manners. Muchembled modifies the scope of this explanation by showing that the process was often urban. Cities were a "third way" between the dominant universe of the aristocrats and that of the peasants. With respect to violence, public places were often better supervised in the cities. Prosperous cities could not tolerate violence without hurting their reputation. Cities enjoyed their golden age until the middle of the sixteenth century, when they were caught in a pincer movement by the nation-state.

19. Gabriel Ardant, *Histoire de l'impot* (Fayard, 1971). Ardant says that "no government of any Mediterranean city gave birth to a representative regime, whose very possibility could not be conceived by theoreticians of political science in Antiquity."

20. The history of the Tudors shows how this dynamic was applied. To increase its revenues, and incidentally to remarry, Henry VIII broke with the pope and appropriated the inviting wealth of the Church. This allowed him to overcome his own budgetary constraint, but it weakened his legitimacy, making it still more necessary to obtain the consent of Parliament. His daughter Elizabeth got out of her own budget problems by commissioning pirate enterprises that paid well, which made her relations with Parliament less conflictual, and which would be an alternative to the constitution of a strong bureaucracy capable of raising taxes.

21. The principal merit of the Glorious Revolution of 1688 was to put an end to English civil wars. It remained a revolution from above, without immediate bearing on the people with respect to democratic rights.

22. Voltaire marveled at the British Revolution: "The blood of Charles I was still warm when the British Parliament, although essentially composed of fanatics, voted the famous Navigation Act." (The Navigation Act, passed in 1651, instituted intellectual property.)

23. Jean-Jacques Rosenthal has also criticized the idea that British growth originated with taxable property rights. For him, it is the opposite. To save money, English aristocrats who were landowners often blocked investments that would have been useful, especially in the domain of irrigation. The debate between the supporters of North and Weingast, who put institutional reform at the heart of the British dynamic, and their opponents, who insist on other fundamental factors like science or education, is far from exhausted. For the views of the former camp, see Avner Greif, *Institutions and the Path to the Modern Economy: Lessons from Medieval Trade* (Cambridge University Press, 2000). The opposite camp includes Gregory Clark; see his *Farewell to Alms* (Princeton University Press, 2007). Comparison between Chinese development and European development offers another terrain for confrontation between the two schools of thought.

———

24. Jared Diamond, in *Guns, Germs, and Steel* (Norton, 1997), emphasizes the role played by the export of its epidemics in the military successes of Europe overseas.

25. The term "political economy" was invented in 1615 by Antoine de Montchrestien, a writer who belonged to a school called *mercantilism*. For mercantilists, commerce and industry were the sources of wealth, and they were favored by what today we would call an industrial and protectionist policy. Mercantilists neglected the agricultural question, for which they would be reproached in the eighteenth century by the Physiocrats.

26. Richard Cantillon's *Essai sur la nature du commerce en general* was published in London in 1755, although it had been written in French around 1730. It was reissued in 1952.

27. This long-term view of history evidently leaves aside the fact that certain civilizations raised themselves (some for a long while) above the Malthusian trap before being caught up in it. For the historian, these exceptional times obviously have more weight than the monotonous rule that submerges all of them.

28. English incomes would more than double after the Great Plague before coming slowly back to their initial level.

29. See Clark, *Farewell to Alms*.

30. Another explanation relates to the fact that a civilization may attain a resplendent summit before falling back into the Malthusian trap. The memory it leaves in the annals of history will be of its best years, not of its decline.

31. To read anthropologists, the infinite variety of arrangements governing sexual life never seems truly linked to the demographic question. This observation was made by Paul Yonnet in *Le Recul de la mort* (Gallimard, 2006). In seventeenth-century France, a woman who married at age 20 had 9.1 children on average. In England, the country with the lowest birth rate, women who married by 20 had

7.6 children. In both cases, couples did not seem to have a contraceptive strategy. Premature births did not reduce the number of children later brought into the world. The reason why European fertility is on average lower than the biological maximum is to be sought outside the couple. Late marriage (or none) is the rule for a significant number of women. Late marriage is often due to the difficulty of finding a home. So there is indeed a feedback of the economic cycle on the demographic cycle. But as soon as the material condition improves, marriage age is advanced and the Malthusian trap closes in on growing societies.

32. The reasons for the French demographic slowdown have long been attributed to the Napoleonic Civil Code, which obliged equal sharing of an inheritance, which pushed parents to reduce the number of children in order not to break up their property. But in fact the French demographic slowdown preceded the creation of the Civil Code, although this line of argument remains valid: Wanting to treat their children equally, even before the law made it an obligation to do so, the French reduced their number.

33. There is a debate among historians about dating the process. The first estimates of British economic growth offered by Phyllis Deane and W. A. Cole in *British Economic Growth, 1688–1959: Trends and Structure* (Cambridge University Press, 1962) show an abrupt spurt. Between 1760 and 1800, the increase in per capita revenue was 0.5 percent per year. From 1800 to 1830, it rose to 1.6 percent. The new data offered by N. F. R. Crafts in *British Economic Growth during the Industrial Revolution* (Oxford University Press, 1985) reduce the figures by two-thirds. Growth was only 0.17 percent per year from 1700 to 1800. It went up to 0.5 percent from 1800 to 1830. According to Crafts, not until the period 1830–1870 did it approach 2 percent per year. However, there is less disagreement over industrial growth itself. Deane and Cole say it went from 1.2 percent to 4 percent between the two periods; Crafts puts it from 1.96 percent to 3 percent. So the disagreement relates less to industrial growth than to its impact on overall growth. The British economy saw its structure modified abruptly. The share of agricultural employment decreased from 61 percent in 1700 to

53 percent in 1760 to 41 percent in 1800 to 29 percent in 1841. Within the industrial sector, modern industries cannibalized the older ones (leather, wool, linen). The effect of industry on the economy as a whole did not really become palpable until the nineteenth century, when industrial employment went from one-third of the male workforce in 1800 to nearly one-half in 1840. See the summary given by Findlay and O'Rourke in *Power and Plenty*.

34. See Patrick Verley, *La Révolution industrielle* (Gallimard "Folio," 1997).

35. See Francois Caron, *Le Résistible Déclin des societiés industrielles* (Perrin, 1985).

36. Joel Mokyr, *The Gift of Athena: Historical Origins of the Knowledge Economy* (Princeton University Press, 2002).

37. Electricity illustrates how experimentation in new technologies and basic science worked together. Faraday demonstrated the possibility of generating electricity by mechanical means in 1831. But it was not until the 1870s that the electrical revolution took place. Edison, one of the pioneers, was not himself a scientist, but employed Francis Upton, who had a PhD in engineering, and Herman Claudius, who had a doctorate in electricity. As in the case of the steam engine, the basic scientific knowledge would not be enlarged until 20 years later, when the theory of electrons was elaborated. But as in the case of thermodynamics, it was these scientific discoveries that made it possible to take the initial discoveries farther and to avoid their collapsing.

38. Crop rotation, developed in Holland, was established in the eighteenth century. This agricultural revolution explains the fascination of Physiocrats for agriculture, which gave a respite in the eighteenth century, but its effects were insufficient to cope with a doubling of the population.

39. In 1815, 60 percent of the textile production in cotton was exported. In parallel, the industry progressed 235 percent between 1780 and 1831, twice as fast as the GDP. On these points, see Findlay and O'Rourke, *Power and Plenty*.

---

40. Pierre Rosanvallon analyzes this anteriority in *Le Capitalisme utopique* (Éditions du Seuil, 1989).

41. "Pride, envy and cupidity are the three sparks that enflame the heart of man." —Dante, *Inferno*, VI, 74–5.

42. Marx, *Capital*, III X, 34.

43. The Englishman Alfred Marshall and the Frenchman Leon Walras are among the founders of neoclassical theory.

44. The industrial reserve army is thus not necessary to understand the origin of profit. The possibility of full employment doesn't imply its necessity, however. Keynes' work, which I examine in chapter 7, explains this logic.

45. Robert Solow, "A Contribution to the Theory of Economic Growth," *Quarterly Journal of Economics* 70, no. 1 (1956): 65–94.

46. Michael Kremer, "Population Growth and Technological Change: One Million BC to 1990," *Quarterly Journal of Economics* 108, no. 3 (1993): 681–716.

47. Paul Romer's principal works are "Crazy Explanations for the Productivity Slowdown," *NBER Macroeconomics Annual* 2 (1987): 163–202, "Capital Accumulation in the Theory of Long Run Growth," in *Modern Business Cycle Theory*, ed. R. Burns (Harvard University Press, 1991), and "Increasing Returns and Long Run Growth," *Journal of Political Economy* 94, no. 5 (1986): 1002–1037. The other founding article of the theory of endogenous growth is Robert Lucas, "On the Mechanics of Economic Development," *Journal of Monetary Economics* 22, no. 1 (1988): 3–42.

48. See Joseph Schumpeter, *Capitalism, Socialism and Democracy* (Harper, 1942). The revival of Schumpeter's theories of growth owes much to the work of Philippe Aghion and Peter Howitt (*Endogenous Growth*, MIT Press, 1997) and to that of Gene Grossman and Elhanan Helpman (*Innovation and Growth in the Global Economy*, MIT Press, 1995). An article by Aghion, Bloom, Blundell, Griffith, and

Howitt ("Competition and Innovation: An Inverted-U Relationship," *Quarterly Journal of Economic* 120, no. 2, 2005: 701–728) moderates the Schumpeterian enthusiasm for monopolies by showing that too large a gap between the leader and imitators can discourage innovation, for lack of opponents.

NOTES TO PART II

1. On these points, see Christian Baechler, *L'Allemagne de Weimar* (Fayard, 2007) and Heinrich Winkler, *Germany: The Long Road West*, volume 1, tr. A. Sager (Oxford University Press, 2006), p. 252.

2. Winkler, *Germany*, volume 1, p. 282.

3. Baechler, *L'Allemagne de Weimar*.

4. In 1910, 60 percent of Germans lived in towns with populations of more than 2,000, as opposed to 36.1 percent in 1871, and 21.3 percent in cities of more than 100,000, versus 4.8 percent in 1871.

5. Baechler, *L'Allemagne de Weimar*.

6. Many historians and sociologists have emphasized this gap between the traditional value system of Prussian society and the developments of modern society as a possible cause of the rise of totalitarianism. See Ian Kershaw, *The Nazi Dictatorship: Problems and Perspectives of Interpretation* (Arnold, 1985).

7. The index of industrial production (based on 100 in 1928) was 98 in 1913, rising to 37 in 1919, and to 70 in 1922.

8. The expiration in January 1925 of the most favored nation clause (given without reciprocity to the Allies by the Treaty of Versailles) also contributed to the regain of confidence.

9. The index of industrial production went from 100 in 1929 to 58 in 1932 and 66 in 1933.

10. In July 1932, only one-seventh of Catholic voters voted for it, whereas more than 50 percent of non-Catholics voters did. Catholic resistance weakened in March 1932, but the affinity of non-Catholics for the Nazi Party remained twice as high per capita. A little less decisive is the contrast between towns and the country (where the NSDAP did more recruiting). In July 1932, 34 percent of small-town voters voted NSDAP, but only 28 percent of voters in large towns.

11. Winkler, *Germany*, volume 2 (Oxford University Press, 2007), p. 576.

12. Lionel Robbins, *The Great Depression* (1934; Books for Libraries Press, 1976), p. 53.

13. John Kenneth Galbraith, *The Great Crash, 1929* (Houghton Mifflin, 1979), 77.

14. The National Bureau of Economic Research, calculating the data from the period, shows that the economy had weakened at the start of the summer of 1929. Steel production declined from June on. In October, the index of industrial production was at 117; four months earlier it had been at 126. House building had been decreasing for several years, and weakened even more in 1929. See Bernard Gazier, *La Crise de 1929* (Presses Universitaires de France, 1985).

15. Peter Temin, *Lessons from the Great Depression* (MIT Press, 1989).

16. Milton Friedman and Anna Schwartz, *A Monetary History of the United States, 1867–1960* (Princeton University Press, 1963).

17. The sequence described echoes the analysis offered at the time by the economist Irving Fisher, who in 1933 talked about "debt deflation." Fisher emphasized the impact of the decrease in prices on the solvency of borrowers. Between 1929 and 1933, retail prices decreased by one-third, and wholesale prices by 40 percent. Businesses desperate to find buyers, starved of liquidity, slashed their sales prices to attract customers. In value, activity therefore contracted twice, once as a result of the decrease in activity and once as a result of the decrease in prices.

A household whose income and debt were both worth 100 in 1929 found itself three years later with a debt still worth 100, but an income that was worth only 30. In relation to the household income or the business sales figures, debt became three times heavier to carry than it had been before the crisis. Households and businesses that could no longer honor their debts went into default. To take an extreme example, 60 percent of the households in Cleveland defaulted on their mortgages. The difficulties of households were shared by businesses, especially small ones.

18. J. M. Keynes, *The General Theory of Employment, Interest and Money* (1936; Harcourt, 1968).

19. Keynes, *Essays in Persuasion* (1936; Harcourt, 1964), p. 46.

20. Here Keynes revives Malthus, who had held a view opposite to that of David Ricardo. Malthus' reasoning was as follows: "Workers eat, capitalists save, property owners spend. If the property owners were to disappear, the capitalist machine would lead to an indefinite accumulation of wealth that nobody would ever consume. . . . It is not illogical to deduce that someday accumulation will be interrupted, for want of outlets." Ricardo's answer to Malthus was rather dogmatic: "Mr. Malthus seems to forget that saving is necessarily spending." For Ricardo, if agents save, this means in effect either that they are buying shares or that they are buying (and hoarding) gold. If it is shares, they are issued either by the government to finance its deficits, hence its expenditures, or else by businesses to finance their investments. In both cases, saving finances expenditure. If people buy gold and hoard it, Ricardo explains to Malthus, then it would be like buying jewels, which changes nothing about Say's Law.

21. Jean Fourastié, *Les Trentes Glorieuses* (Fayard, 1979; Hachette, ed. D. Cohen, 2004). This chapter borrows from my previous book *The Misfortunes of Prosperity* (MIT Press, 1995).

22. William Baumol, *Performing Arts: The Economic Dilemma* (MIT Press, 1968).

———

23. Philippe Askenazy, *Les Désordres du travail* (Éditions du Seuil, 2004).

24. Eric Maurin, *L'Égalité des possibles* (Éditions du Seuil, 2002).

25. To imitate a scheme of growth is easier than to invent one. That doesn't mean that it suffices to want to do so in order to be able to. Today China and India are embarked on a scheme of catching up with the leading countries, but analysts have long thought that this catching up was impossible. In the European case, many productivity missions were sent to the United States. Today, in the Chinese case, direct investments play a great role.

26. Robert Delorme and Christine Andre, *L'État et l'économie* (Éditions du Seuil, 1983).

27. See Brigitte Dormont, *Les Dépenses de santé, une augmentation salutaire?* (Éditions Rue d'Ulm, 2009).

28. Kenneth Arrow, "Uncertainty and the Welfare Economics of Medical Care," *American Economic Review* 53, no. 5 (1963): 941–973.

29. These studies were cited by Henry Aaron in his survey "Economic Aspects of the Role of Government in Health Care," in *Health, Economics, and Health Economics*, ed. J. Van der Gaag and M. Perlman (North-Holland, 1971).

30. Paul Samuelson, "An Exact Consumption Loan Model With or Without the Social Contrivance of Money," *Journal of Political Economy* 66, no. 6 (1958): 467–482; Maurice Allais, *Économie et Intéret* (Imprimerie Nationale, 1947).

31. Richard A. Easterlin, "Does Economic Growth Improve the Human Lot?" in *Nations and Households in Economic Growth: Essays in Honor of Moses Abramovich*, ed. P. David and M. Reder (Academic Press, 1974). For more recent updates, see Richard Layard, *Happiness: Lessons from a New Science* (Penguin, 2005); Bruno Frey, *Happiness: A Revolution in Economics* (MIT Press, 2008).

32. Karl Marx, *Wage, Labor and Capital* (1847).

33. Envy is not the only issue in the comparison with others. Albert Hirschman compares the consumer to a driver stuck in a traffic jam. When the neighboring lane is free, he is at first soothed, for he sees the promise of being off and away soon. But if he remains stuck in a lane that is not moving, he gets irritated and may become violent, changing lanes regardless of the danger. Thus one speaks of the "tunnel effect" when the comparison with another enables inferring information about the field of possibilities. Knowing that your neighbor has a high-definition TV gives you the desire to have one, quite simply because you know they exist. If you don't have the money to buy one, hatred of the other may arise. For a review of the literature, see Andrew Clark and Claudia Senik, *27 Questions D'Economie Contermporaine*, ed. P. Askenazy and D. Cohen (Albin Michel, 2008).

34. Jean-Pierre Vernant, *The Universe, the Gods, and Mortals*, tr. L. Asher (Harper, 2001), p. 56ff.

35. N. D. Kondratieff, "The Long Waves in Economic Life," translated by Guy Daniels from a 1925 article in *The Long Wave Cycle*, ed. J. Snyder (Richardson and Snyder, 1984). This chapter borrows from my book *The Misfortunes of Prosperity*.

36. Gaston Imbert, *Des mouvements de longue durée Kondratieff* (La Pensée Universitaire, 1959).

37. See the collection *La Longue Stagnation en France: l'autre grande dépression 1873–1897*, ed. Y. Breton, A. Broder, and M. Lutfalla (Economica, 1997).

38. Imbert, *Des mouvements de longue durée Kondratieff*.

39. Alex L. Macfie, "The Outbreak of War and the Trade Cycle," *Economic History*, supplement to *Economic Journal*, February 1958.

40. Joseph Schumpeter, *Imperialism and Social Classes* (Kelley, 1951).

41. Paul Kennedy, *The Rise and Fall of the Great Powers: Economic Change and Military Conflict 1500–2000* (Random House, 1989).

42. Philippe Martin, Thierry Mayer, and Mathias Thoenig, *La mondialisation est-elle un facteur de paix?* (Éditions Rue de l'Ulm, 2006).

43. Albert Hirschman, *The Passions and the Interests: Political Arguments for Capitalism Before its Triumph* (Princeton University Press, 1977), p. 45.

44. Albert Hirschman, *Shifting Involvements: Private Interest and Public Action* (Princeton University Press, 1980).

45. Ernest Gellner, *Nations and Nationalism*, second edition (Cornell University Press, 1983), p. 22.

46. Ernst Cassirer, *The Myth of the State*, quoted in Winkler, *Germany*, volume 2, p. 107.

NOTES TO PART III

1. Max Weber, *The Protestant Ethic and the Spirit of Capitalism* (1905).

2. Kenneth Pomeranz, *The Great Divergence: China, Europe, and the Making of the Modern World Economy* (Princeton University Press, 2000).

3. Joseph Needham, *Science and Civilization in China* (Cambridge University Press, 1954); abridged by Robert Temple in *The Genius of China* (André Deutsch, 2007).

4. The idea of a separation between the social capital of a company, its moral persona, and the physical person who holds it did not occur in China, where merchant capital remained associated with a family. In fact familial capitalism of the "Asiatic" type remained long dominant in Europe, too, except in certain sectors. Europeans used limited share companies mainly for overseas commerce, distinguishing the moral persona of the firm from the persons of its owners. By any account, England's industrial development in textiles or metallurgy wasn't financed by the financial markets; instead, the low investment cost was easily

---

borne by families. On this point, see Jack Goody, *The East in the West* (Cambridge University Press, 1996).

5. Political fragmentation did not contribute to reducing European tax revenue, as was sometimes thought, due to a "fiscal dumping" between states. The British tax rate fluctuated between 15 percent and 20 percent, according to the authors, and was among the highest in Europe between 1688 and 1800. The Indian Empire of the Moguls would require fiscal resources comparable with those of England itself, but it was the exception. China collected only half as much in taxes. Nor can one say that the British state was more "responsible" than others about expenditures. The two absolutist states of continental Europe—Spain and France—had at their disposal much more meager fiscal resources. Apparently, 83 percent of British public expenditure was for the military.

6. Migratory movement toward more fertile and less densely populated lands remained much slower in Europe than in China. While the advantage for a young Englishman in migrating to New England was considerable (ten years more in life expectancy around 1700, for example), migrations remained very sparse for a long time.

7. Progress in metallurgy enabled the Chinese to produce (starting in the eleventh century) 125,000 tons of cast iron, a figure not attained in England until 700 years later.

8. David Landes, "Why Europe and the West? Why Not China?" *Journal of Economic Perspectives* 20, no. 2 (2006): 3–22.

9. Étienne Balazs, *La Bureaucratie céleste* (Gallimard, 1968); *Chinese Civilization and Bureaucracy: Variations on a Theme*, tr. H. Wright (Yale University Press, 1964).

10. Fernand Braudel, *A History of Civilizations*, tr. R. Mayne (Penguin 1994), p. 198.

11. Erik Izraelewicz, *Quand la Chine change le monde* (Hachette, 2005).

12. Corruption also played a role in the reasons for leaving a gray zone with respect to rural ownership.

13. See Jacqueline Tsai, *La Chine et le luxe* (Odile Jacob, 2008).

14. Most of the lowering in poverty took place in the 1980s. While the Chinese population passed from 981 million in 1980 to 1.162 billion in 1992, the number of poor people declined from a margin of 360–530 million in 1980 to 158–192 million in 1992.

15. See Thomas Vendryes, "Land Rights and Rural-Urban Migration in China," Ecole d'Economie de Paris, summary published in *China Perspectives*, 2008/2.

16. David Smith, *Growling Tiger, Roaring Dragon* (Douglas & McIntyre, 2007).

17. The barrier limiting to 40 percent the share of capital that foreign investors could hold was lowered. Foreign ownership was permitted up to 51 percent, timidly at first, in only 34 industries. But ownership of 100 percent of the capital was authorized for foreign investments designed for zones dedicated to exports (as would be done in China).

18. Christophe Jaffrelot, *La Démocratie en Inde* (Fayard, 1998).

19. Francis Fukuyama, *The End of History and the Last Man* (Macmillan, 1992; Free Press, 2006).

20. Samuel Huntington, *The Clash of Civilizations and the Remaking of World Order* (Simon & Schuster, 1996).

21. Fukuyama has often replied to his critics that he did not ignore the dangers of the current world, but the problem that he was studying was based on the available political models. The important question that remains is whether this model has any predictive value.

22. Arjun Appadurai, *Fear of Small Numbers: Essay on the Geography of Anger* (Duke University Press, 2006), p. 22.

23. Amy Chua, *The World on Fire: How Exporting Free Market Democracy Breeds Ethnic Hatred and Global Instability* (Doubleday, 2003).

24. Ibid., p. 5.

25. Ibid, p. 10.

26. Appadurai, *Fear of Small Numbers*, p. 45.

27. This is the interpretation given of the French Revolution, which, unlike the English Revolution of 1688, established the idea of an equality of rights and duties among all citizens. In the English case, these rights would remain long confined to an elite who dealt with the monarchy as one power with another.

28. Ian Kershaw, *The Nazi Dictatorship: Problems and Perspectives of Interpretation* (Bloomsbury, 1985). Kershaw adds that once in power, the Nazis scarcely changed the rules of the social game: "The private reserves—major industry, the public service, and the army—continued to recruit most of their leaders from the same social strata as before 1933." This also explains the increase in violence engendered against minorities. "The disappointment of many social aspirations under the Third Reich was compensated for, up to a certain point, by the channeling of energies into an activism against powerless and subject minorities, against pariahs excluded for social or racial reasons from the 'national community.'"

29. René Girard, *The Scapegoat*, tr. Y. Freccero (Johns Hopkins University Press, 1986). Originally published in French in 1982.

30. Paul Collier, *The Bottom Billion* (Oxford University Press, 2007).

31. Daron Acemoglu, Simon Johnson, and James A. Robinson, "The Colonial Origins of Comparative Development: An Empirical Investigation," *American Economic Review* 91, no. 5 (2001): 1369–1401.

32. This observation was made by Edward Glaeser, Rafael La Porta, Florencio Lopez de Silanes, and Andrei Shleifer in "Do Institutions Cause Growth?"

(*Journal of Economic Growth* 9, no. 3, 2004: 271–303). Written in response to Ace-moglu et al., the article shows that the institutional legacy is much more erratic than anticipated. The leaders' political opportunism plays just as essential a role.

33. Albert Hirschman, *The Passions and the Interests* (Princeton University Press, 1977).

34. Ian Buruma and Avishai Margalit, *Occidentalism: The West in the Eyes of Its Enemies* (Penguin, 2004).

35. The Ba'athist ideology of the Syrian and Iraqi governments, elaborated in the 1930s and the 1940s, is itself a synthesis of fascism and romantic nostalgia for an organic Arab community. Sak Hursi, one of those who inspired the movement, had studied the German Romantic thinkers Fichte and Herder, who were struggling against the French Enlightenment spirit by opposing to it the concept of "the popular and organic nation rooted in blood and soil."

36. Albert Memmi, *The Colonizer and the Colonized*, preface by J.-P. Sartre, tr. H. Greenfield (Beacon, 1991).

37. Robert Muchembled, *Une Histoire de la violence: De la fin du Moyen Age à nos jours* (Éditions du Seuil, 2008).

38. I am borrowing figures and a line of argument given by Jeffrey Sachs in *Commonwealth* (Penguin, 2008).

39. Lester R. Brown, *Plan B: Rescuing a Planet under Stress and a Civilization in Trouble* (Norton, 2005), p. 11. This is updated annually—e.g., *Plan B 4.0: Mobilizing to Save Civilization* (Norton, 2009).

40. One of the causes of the world's food problems is the fact that food and fuel are in competition for arable land. Between 2000 and 2005, world production of ethanol went from 14 million to 37 million tons. Brazil covers 40 percent of its need in ethanol, derived from sugarcane. It is ridiculous that this industry should be subsidized by governments.

41. In 2005, world production settled at 30.5 billion barrels. Discovery of new deposits was limited to 7.5 billion.

42. The chemical equation of global warming is itself relatively simple. A fossil fuel is constituted of carbon and hydrogen in variable proportions. Coal is mostly carbon, with a little hydrogen and it is the most dangerous fossil from the warming standpoint. Petroleum is essentially CH_2, one carbon atom for two of hydrogen. Natural gas is formed of CH_2. When a fossil fuel burns, the carbon is combined with oxygen to form CO_2, carbon dioxide, while the hydrogen combines with oxygen to form H_2O, water. Burning a tree produces almost the same effect.

43. In 1988 the World Meteorological Organization and the UN Environmental Program created the IPPC, in which all UN and WMO members could take part. The fourth report was presented in 2007 and discussed in detail the causes of global warming and remedies.

44. Brown, *Plan B*, pp. 44–45.

45. Ibid, p. 109.

46. Ibid., 228.

47. The cost in terms of electricity of reducing carbon emissions in relation to current tendencies might be between \$10 and \$50 per ton of CO_2 or from \$1 to \$5 dollars per kilowatt-hour (Sachs, *Commonwealth*).

48. "Credibility" emerged as an important term at this time. To be "credible" is to do what you said you were going to do, even if it is disagreeable. Nuclear deterrence was credible if the enemy thought that you would not hesitate to push the button, even if that would cause gigantic losses. A central bank is credible if one can count on the fact that it will conduct a strict policy when needed, even if this should cause the unpopularity of leaders. As soon as an institution like the Fed loses its credibility, agents bet on the worst:

repeated devaluations, an inflation that accelerates, and so on. The sole fact of these expectations makes it much more difficult for a central bank to regulate the economy thereafter.

49. Peter Sloterdijk, *Rage and Time: A Psychopolitical Investigation*, tr. M. Wenning (Columbia University Press, 2010), p. 216.

50. A good example of the mutation caused by a finance market is the American International Group. As an insurance company, it wasn't subject to the same oversight as deposit banks. It was able to create a department of AIG Finances, which found itself the prime operator in credit default swaps, which guaranteed the creditor against the risk of the debtor's bankruptcy. Commercial banks also played this game by developing financial services housed outside their balances in *ad hoc* structures that cheerfully bought the risky credit of subprimes. This was made as legal as possible by profiting from holes in the regulation system, but also from a certain laxity in the authorities, which should very well have perceived the scheme if they had been more vigilant. But they did not. Why? No doubt because they had been convinced by the climate of ambient ideas, this new paradigm of a market left entirely to itself, according to which all financial operations could regulate themselves. Without that pervasive paradigm, the regulatory authorities would have begun to ask to open the account books.

51. One of the mistakes in calculations related to the hypothesis that there never had been a major American mortgage crisis at the national level, but only regional crises. See Andre Orléan, *De l'euphorie à la panique: penser la crise financière* (Éditions rue d'Ulm, 2009).

52. Piketty and Saez, "The Evolution of Top Incomes: A Historical and International Perspective" (http://elsa.berkeley.edu/~saez/piketty-saezAEAPP06 .pdf).

53. Voltaire is caricaturing Leibniz and his principle of "sufficient reason." Upset by the Lisbon earthquake, Voltaire is revolted by the idea that an evil might

necessarily be the counterpart of a blessing. Pangloss incarnates this vision of considering that the world is the best possible one, despite all its defects.

54. Andrew Haldane, "Rethinking the Financial Network" (http://www .bankofengland.co.uk/publications/speeches/2009/speech386.pdf).

55. I develop all these points in *Three Lectures on Post-Industrial Society*, tr. W. McCuaig (MIT Press, 2009).

56. Huntington, *The Clash of Civilizations*, p. 58.

57. Françoise Benhamou, *L'Economie du star-system* (Odile Jacob, 2002).

58. Tyler Cowen, *Creative Destruction* (Princeton University Press, 2002).

59. Alan Krueger notes that the salary of performing artists derived from the organization of world tours has increased 82 percent in ten years. Fans want to see their idols: it is the demand that keeps prices up. The performer Prince offers his CDs during his concerts, which give another reason to come and hear him. David Bowie is the singer who has best theorized this evolution; the artist should put himself on stage in the strict sense, for he is the material part of his immateriality.

60. *Livres Hebdo* study, May 19, 2006.

61. On certain evenings, the same American producer is present on both prime French channels—for example, with *CSI* and *FBI: Missing*.

62. Africa is the continent most lagging in the demographic transition. Even in this case, though, it has already begun, with UN experts foreseeing the number of children per woman as 2.5 in 2050.

63. I develop this point in *Globalization and Its Enemies*, tr. J. Barker (MIT Press, 2007).

64. See Olivier Mongine, "Puissance du virtuel, déchainements des possibles et dévalorisation du monde: Retour sur des remarques de Jean-Toussaint Desanti," *Esprit*, August 2004.

———

NOTES TO CONCLUSION

1. Robert Muchembled, *Une Histoire de la violence: De la fin du Moyen Age à nos jours* (Éditions du Seuil, 2008).

2. Thinking of the risk of a tragic outcome becomes healthy if one wants to avoid that fate. On this point see Jean-Pierre Dupuy, *Pour un autotrophisme éclairé* (Éditions du Seuil, 2002). Literature has gradually adopted this theme. See Cormac McCarthy's apocalyptic novel *The Road* (Random House 2006), which won a Pulitzer Prize and was made into a film.

Index

Great Depression, 63–73
Greco-Roman civilization, 8, 9
Greed, 164–166
Greenhouse gases, 148
Greenspan, Alan, 64, 166
Growth
  addiction to, 90–94
  periods of high and low, 101–106
  perpetual, 41–50, 79–81, 90–94,
    185, 186
  slowing of, 89, 90
  war and, 101–106, 186

Hansen, Alvin, 101
Happiness, 90–92, 97, 103–106,
  187
Health, spending on, 85, 86
Hegel, G. W. F., 57
Hirschman, Albert, 42, 103, 104,
  105, 137
Hitler, Adolf, 58, 61
Hoover, Herbert, 68
Huntington, Samuel, 131, 132,
  138
Hyperinflation, 59

Iceland, 156
Imbert, Gaston, 101
Immaterial production, 176, 177
Imperialism, 101, 102
India, 121–130

Industrial reserve army, 45, 46
Industrial Revolution, 33–40
  new, 153–155
Inequality, 165, 173
Innovation, industrial, 35
Interconnection, economic, 169–171
Intergovernmental Panel on Climate
  Change, 148, 149
Internet, 187
Invisible hand, 49
Islam, 139

Japan, 117, 139
Jews, 58
Jones, Eric, 18
Joule, James Prescott, 37

Kay, John, 34
Kennedy, Paul, 102
Kershaw, Ian, 135
Keynesianism, 158, 159
Keynes, John Maynard, 53, 55, 66,
  67, 70–73, 83, 84, 101, 158–160,
  169
Kondratieff, Nicolas, 75
Koyré, Alexander, 17
Kremer, Michael, 48
Kyoto Protocol, 152, 153

Landes, David, 36
Land, privatization of, 117